What It Means
to be as
Wise
as a
Serpent

Dag Heward-Mills

Parchment House

WHAT IT MEANS TO BE AS WISE AS A SERPENT

First published 2015 by Parchment House
12th Printing 2019

⁷Find out more about Dag Heward Mills at:

Healing Jesus Campaign
Email: evangelist@daghewardmills.org
Website: www.daghewardmills.org
Facebook: Dag Heward-Mills
Twitter: @EvangelistDag

ISBN : 978-1-61395-560-4

Contents

CHAPTER 1

The Wisdom of Serpents

. . . be ye therefore wise as serpents, and harmless as doves.

Matthew 10:16

Serpents Are Wise

It is not strange that men fear snakes. It is also not strange if people have a proper respect for snakes. It is a fact that snakes are amazing creatures, superbly surviving and multiplying in spite of the generalized hatred that exists towards them.

If Jesus had not spoken about the wisdom of serpents we may have overlooked the superior wisdom that they live by. Because Jesus pointed out the wisdom of a serpent, all of us must pay special attention to these creatures and learn what we can from them. So, what is the wisdom of a serpent? What makes a serpent wise?

Would you not want to find the wisdom that would make you flourish more than all your colleagues?

Would you not want to find the wisdom that could make you successful in the face of strong opposition and hatred?

Would you not want to have the wisdom that would make you flourish through all the changing scenes of life? After all, how many people are able to stay rich and prosperous through all seasons of life?

Would you not want the wisdom that would make people fear you and treat you with proper respect? Do you not want the wisdom that will make you quietly accomplish all your goals in this life?

I am sure you want such wisdom. Indeed, that is the wisdom of the serpent! That is why Jesus said we must be wise as serpents.

Seven Reasons Why Serpents Are Considered Wise

1. Serpents are considered to be wise because they have multiplied and flourished more than any other wild animal.

2. Serpents are considered to be wise because they have continued to exist in an ever-modernising world. You will notice that many wild animals are becoming extinct in our modern world.

3. Serpents are considered to be wise because they have been able to flourish even though they are hated by everyone.

4. Serpents are considered to be wise because they evoke fear and respect in human beings. Human beings do not fear and respect many animals but they fear and respect snakes.

5. Serpents are considered to be wise because of their ability to live in every continent and every part of the world.

6. Serpents are considered to be wise because of their ability to function in every sphere; on land, in the sea, in fresh water and even in the air.

7. Serpents are considered to be wise because of their ability to accomplish their goals in this world. In spite of all the odds stacked against the snakes, they are able to live, eat and multiply.

To be wise, you must think, meditate and ponder over facts, truths and statements. You cannot just gloss over deep sayings that mean so much. When Jesus said, "Be wise as serpents", he was giving a dark saying; a saying that is full of wisdom, meaning and guidance. Every chapter of this book contains one aspect of the great wisdom of a serpent that has made it more successful than any other wild animal found in the zoo.

Have you ever thought about the fact that there are no lions roaming around near your house? But there are probably snakes in your area. At least, I have seen snakes in every house I have ever lived in. Lions are simply non-existent in your area. They have been wiped out because they do not operate by the wisdom of the serpent. They operate by another kind of wisdom – the wisdom of a lion.

The wisdom of a lion makes us have a proper respect and fear for lions. But the wisdom of a lion has not enabled the lion to flourish and multiply successfully in cities all over the world. The population of lions is dwindling! Lions are becoming extinct! Snakes, on the other hand, are mysteriously found in every city and neighbourhood. In that sense, the snake is wiser than the lion because it has prevailed, flourished and prospered whereas the lions have become fewer and are nearing extinction.

CHAPTER 2

Masters of Non-Dependent Living

Make it your ambition to lead a quiet life, to mind your own business and to work with your hands, just as we told you, so that your daily life may win the respect of outsiders and SO THAT YOU WILL NOT BE DEPENDENT ON ANYBODY.

1 Thessalonians 4:11-12 (NIV)

Serpents Are Wise Because They Do Not Depend On Outsiders

A leader must not depend on anyone in order to command the respect of outsiders. A minister must work hard in order to avoid begging in all its forms. Begging is begging whether presidents, politicians or pastors are doing it! Begging is begging even when it is given respectable descriptions such as "seeking investors," "seeking aid" or "attending donor conferences." The alternative to depending on others is to mind your own business and work with your own hands.

Why do you go around begging and asking for things? Have you never read when David said, "… I have not seen the righteous forsaken, nor his seed begging bread" (Psalm 37:25)? Do you not feel ashamed to be living your life hoping for someone to give you something? Do you think outsiders have any respect for you when you depend on them continually? They do not! Read the scripture carefully and meditate on it. "Make it your ambition to lead a quiet life, to mind your own business and to work with your hands, just as we told you, so that your daily life may win the respect of outsiders and so that you will not be dependent on anybody" (1 Thessalonians 4:11 NIV).

Snakes demonstrate that they are masters of independent living. They are able to survive on their own from the day they are born. To be wise as a serpent you must be able to be independent or non-dependent. It is a sorry sight to watch presidents of poor nations going around seeking gifts and loans from richer countries.

Unfortunately, many nations that were colonised have not been able to survive without their colonial masters. They are simply not capable of independence. Many poor countries are failed states, incapable of governing themselves! They fought for independence but they are not independent at all. They celebrate independence every year when they should actually mourn their continued dependence!

Hopelessly incapable leaders have governed nations and led them on a downward spiral into deepening poverty. The fact that leaders are incapable of building roads between two cities, providing electricity, water, schools and hospitals is the evidence of poor and incapable leadership. To the leaders of some poor nations, leadership of a nation means going around to beg for money.

Serpents, on the other hand, are independent from the day they are born and are able to successfully live apart from their parents. Most snakes can kill from the day they are born and often live alone from the first day of their lives. Unlike certain nations that need handouts and gifts from other nations in order to survive, serpents need no assistance and are able to launch out into a successful independent life.

How To Demonstrate That You Are Capable of Independence

1. If you are wise as a serpent you will live your life not expecting money, gifts, grants, donations or even loans.

   And Abram said to the king of Sodom, I have lift up mine hand unto the LORD, the most high God, the possessor of heaven and earth,

   That I will not take from a thread even to a shoelatchet, and that I will not take any thing that is thine, LEST THOU SHOULDEST SAY, I HAVE MADE ABRAM RICH:

   Genesis 14:22-23

   Abraham did not need anybody to make him rich. In fact, he did not want anybody to think that they had made him rich.

   It is children who always expect that Mummy and Daddy will give them something to solve their problems. When someone is incapable of independent living, he often expects people to give him something. Many people look to America and England, expecting to receive something. The fact that you even think that Americans and Europeans will come to your aid shows that you are incapable of an independent life.

You must not expect that any outsider will make you rich. Why do you want somebody to give you something? Why are you always looking, hoping and expecting a gift, a loan or a handout? Indeed, incapable leaders throw dust in your eyes when they announce that they are seeking loans to embark on projects. Often, there is no need for the loan. There is simply a need to cut out waste, corruption and poor management of resources. These bad leaders fool the masses with their talk about acquiring loans. But those who can see through the smoke and the fog can tell that there is actually no need for a loan.

You must lead your life in a way that will make you independent of an external donor. Hopelessly incapable leaders are always happy to go for donor conferences to hear what grants and gifts will be dished out to them. Amazingly, some of these leaders fall asleep at these donor meetings because they are simply out of their depth when it comes to leadership.

2. If you are wise as a serpent you will be a master of your own life and will not need anyone to build things for you.

Your wisdom will lead you to rise up and build for yourself. This is why a man is said to be wise when he has built things. The inability to build reveals the lack of wisdom. If you are wise as a serpent you will rise up and build the things you need. Solomon built many things himself. He built houses, planted vineyards, made gardens and orchards and planted trees of all kinds of fruits and made pools.

I made me great works; I builded me houses; I planted me vineyards:

I made me gardens and orchards, and I planted trees in them of all kind of fruits:

I made me pools of water, to water therewith the wood that bringeth forth trees:

Ecclesiastes 2:4-6

A pastor who runs a church expecting someone to come along and build a building for him is incapable of mature, non-dependent leadership. Until you learn to look at the few resources you have and plan your existence around what you own, you are incapable of mature independent living.

3. If you are wise as a serpent you will not ask for gifts, loans and continually beg for assistance.

You must not ask for gifts or beg for money. When you are as wise as a serpent you know that you are on your own from day one. Every serpent knows this. You must rise up and meet the challenges, knowing that others have encountered the exact same challenges and were able to overcome. The reason why nations receive gifts and aid and loans and never prosper is because that is all they know how to do: ask, beg and plead for gifts, loans and donations. They do not know how to rise up and count their pennies. They do not know how to roll up their sleeves and work with their hands.

People who do not know the history of America think that America became rich by osmosis or some supernatural miracle. The plain hard work of building roads, cities and railways is often lost on the ignorant masses. America was built with sweat and manual labour.

There is a canal in the United States of America that was built in 1825. It was built without engineers and dug out manually by about five thousand workers. This 580-kilometer canal stretched from New York City (from Albany on the Hudson River to Buffalo on Lake Erie) to the middle of America. The canal provided amazingly cheap transportation from the middle of America to the coast. New York City boomed and by 1840 there were many millionaires in that city. This wealth did not come to America by receiving gifts and handouts from outside. It came by the hard work of people who did not look for help from outside.

4. If you are wise as a serpent, you will learn to encourage yourself.

You must not depend on outsiders to encourage you. A person who is capable of living independently will learn to encourage himself because it is wisdom to live without expecting to be encouraged and comforted by another. David encouraged himself in the Lord.

So David and his men came to the city, and, behold, it was burned with fire; and their wives, and their sons, and their daughters, were taken captives.

Then David and the people that were with him lifted up their voice and wept, until they had no more power to weep.

And David's two wives were taken captives, Ahinoam the Jezreelitess, and Abigail the wife of Nabal the Carmelite.

And David was greatly distressed; for the people spake of stoning him, because the soul of all the people was grieved, every man for his sons and for his daughters: BUT DAVID ENCOURAGED HIMSELF IN THE LORD HIS GOD.

1 Samuel 30:3-6

Steps to Independent Living

1. Accept that no one really cares about your condition. Therefore, you must care for yourself. Fight for yourself and strive to rise up independently.

2. Develop a dislike for loans and gifts. Every admirer of gifts and loans is likely to fail in leadership. Many people do not pay back their loans.

3. Do not have an expensive lifestyle. Cut your coat according to your size. Avoid grandiose and expensive things that others may be doing. There are people who do not fear debts and live happily using large sums of money, even though they owe a lot of money. Do not be deceived and do not follow bad examples because it will not end well.

4. Cut out waste. Most poor nations waste half of their resources. That is why they are poor and incapable of developing themselves. They simply have not learnt to prevent wastage and corruption.

5. Learn to do things yourself and with your own hands. Do it yourself. Some people love to sit aloof in an armchair and never roll up their sleeves to work with their own hands. They imagine that they are executives when they are not at that level. They function as the highest kind of executives and do not know much about the practical things that go on.

CHAPTER 3

Masters of Inner Power

And he said, That which cometh out of the man, that defileth the man. FOR FROM WITHIN, out of the heart of men, proceed evil thoughts, adulteries, fornications, murders, thefts, covetousness, wickedness, deceit, lasciviousness, an evil eye, blasphemy, pride, foolishness: All these evil things come from within, and defile the man.

Mark 7:20-23

Serpents Are Wise Because They Have Inner Power

S erpents are wise because they have developed inner power. The great wisdom of the serpent is to have developed internal power that is called venom. Snakes produce saliva from within their mouths just like we all do. The saliva of a snake is its venom. The venom a snake produces within itself is so powerful that it can kill a human being, a lion or even an entire village.

The great power of a snake comes from within. The snake produces saliva from within itself and this saliva is so potent that a drop of it can send you to your grave. Imagine your saliva being so powerful that you could kill someone by spitting at him.

The venom of the king cobra is so deadly that one bite can kill twenty people or one elephant.

The Australian Brown Snake's venom is so powerful that only 1/14,000th of an ounce is needed to kill a human being.

Australia's inland taipan snake (Oxyuranus microlepidotus) is said to possess the strongest venom of any land snake. Fortunately, it seeks unpopulated areas and rarely bites people. Taipan snakes have venom 50 times more toxic than a cobra.

Every man can unleash positive powers or negative powers from within. It is when something comes from deep within that it is powerful. Both positive and negative things gain their power when they are from within and from the heart. Without the heart's involvement every word and physical action is really powerless.

Consider a young lady who is raped by an armed robber. This young lady has had several boyfriends in the past and committed fornication with all of them. She is well known for her immoral and sexual sins. Now, the armed robber asks her to bend over to allow him to rape her in a similar style that she used to have sex with her other boyfriends. After the rape event is over, no one accuses the young lady of having committed fornication or any sin with the armed robber. No one even says she has been immoral or unholy. Why is that? Why are people rather sympathetic to her? Did she not do the exact same things with the armed robber that she did with her other boyfriends?

Why is it that the same physical act is considered to be a sin on one day and on another occasion it is not even considered to be wrong? The answer is simple. She did not bend over of her free will or from her heart. Because these actions did not emanate from her heart, she is considered to be guiltless and sinless.

Jesus taught us that it is only when something comes from within and from the heart that it has power. It is only when preaching comes from the heart that it is powerful. It is only when teaching comes from the heart that it is powerful. It is only when we do things from the heart that they have power. The real power is from within! Read it for yourself!

And he said, That which cometh out of the man, that defileth the man. For FROM WITHIN, out of THE HEART of men, proceed evil thoughts, adulteries, fornications, murders, thefts, covetousness, wickedness, deceit, lasciviousness, an evil eye, blasphemy, pride, foolishness: All these evil things COME FROM WITHIN, AND DEFILE the man.

Mark 7:20-23

The power that comes from within you is the strong force that can do wonders in your life and ministry. It is what comes from within you that determines how powerful you may be. What is on the outside has very little real effect.

Inner Power

To be wise as a serpent you must seriously work on what is within you!

You cannot be used by God if you are not as wise as a serpent. A snake has a lot of power and the power is all internal.

The great wisdom of the serpent is to develop internal power. The great wisdom of the serpent is to fight with internal powers. Work on your hidden internal thinking processes. Your negative thoughts reduce the power within you. A minister must work on his thoughts. Jesus said that the things that defile you come from inside.

When you open your inner life to hidden evil thoughts, hidden deceit, hidden thefts and hidden adultery, all your powers go out and you are like a snake without saliva or venom!

Most aspects of righteousness are hidden. True righteousness is not easy to see because you cannot see the hearts and minds of people. You have to be strong internally so that God can anoint you!

An evil eye, evil thoughts, adulteries, fornications, murders, thefts, covetousness, wickedness, deceit, lasciviousness, blasphemy, pride and foolishness deplete spiritual power and contaminate you.

Internal Powers

The fruit of the Spirit is a product of the inner being. The fruit of the Spirit is the product of the inner being. It is what comes from the inside. Whether you believe it or not, the greatest power that can come out of your life are the fruits and products of the Spirit. The fruits of the Spirit are love, joy, peace, patience, kindness, goodness, faithfulness, gentleness and self-control. Use every opportunity you have to develop these inner qualities.

Which power did Jesus use to influence the whole world? Was it not the power of love, peace and goodness?

But the fruit of the Spirit is love, joy, peace, patience, kindness, goodness, faithfulness, gentleness, self-control; against such things there is no law.

Galatians 5:22-23 (NASB)

Many people mocked at Jesus Christ when He came to this world with the power of love, sacrifice and obedience. Through these inner qualities, Jesus Christ has changed the whole world. Two thousand years after his death and resurrection, the world acknowledges the inner qualities of Jesus Christ by celebrating Christmas. When inner power is developed, then you have real power. Many people laughed at me when I was developing the power of faithfulness and loyalty within my disciples. But it is only by the power of faithfulness and loyalty that a mega church in different locations can be built.

I agree that these inner qualities do not look very powerful. But such is the wisdom of a serpent. A snake may not look very powerful as it lies sleeping in the grass. But it has within its mouth a well-developed and complex power that can kill a truckload of armed soldiers.

Develop Inner Power By Investing in Your Spirit

For he that soweth to his flesh shall of the flesh reap corruption; but he that soweth to the Spirit shall of the Spirit reap life everlasting.

Galatians 6:8

1. **Develop inner power by having regular quiet times with God.** When Jesus had a quiet time with the Lord, an angel was sent to strengthen him. Every time you have a

quiet time with the Lord you can expect to be strengthened spiritually.

And there appeared an angel unto him from heaven, strengthening him.

Luke 22:43

2. **Pray in tongues.** Speaking in tongues builds you up internally. When you speak in tongues you are edified, which means you are built up and charged like a battery.

One who speaks in a tongue EDIFIES himself; but one who prophesies edifies the church.

1 Corinthians 14:4

3. **Meditate on the word of God.** Meditation has a powerful effect on you. It's able to change you from a failure into a success. An inner power is developed within you when you meditate on the word. It is that inner power that makes you successful. Notice how the scripture assures you of success in your life through meditation.

This book of the law shall not depart out of thy mouth; but thou shalt meditate therein day and night, that thou mayest observe to do according to all that is written therein: for then thou shalt make thy way prosperous, and then thou shalt have good success.

Joshua 1:8

4. **Protect your heart from evil contamination.** Your heart is easily contaminated with bitterness, unforgiveness, prejudice, wickedness, revenge, adultery, lust and jealousy. If you do not watch your heart it will soon become a repository of many evils.

Keep thy heart with all diligence; for out of it are the issues of life.

Proverbs 4:23

CHAPTER 4

Masters of the Powers of the Mouth

Out of his mouth go burning torches; Sparks of fire leap forth.

Job 41:19, (NASB)

Serpents Are Wise Because They Use The Power in Their Mouths

S nakes are wise because they use their mouths as weapons to fight, to win and to dominate their enemies. A minister will be wise when he uses his mouth as a weapon to fight, to win and to dominate in the Spirit.

The mouth of a snake is an amazing weapon that it uses very sucessfully. Snakes do not chew their food. Their teeth are good for catching and holding prey, but not suitable for chewing. They have a very flexible lower jaw, the two halves of which are not rigidly attached. They also have numerous other joints in their skull, allowing them to open their mouths wide enough to swallow their prey whole. Snakes are therefore able to swallow their prey whole even if it is larger in diameter than the snake itself. This kind of mouth combined with the venom we have spoken about makes a snake an awesome predator.

Every minister has been given some power in the mouth. Even our salvation comes to us when we open our mouths and confess what we believe with our hearts. "That if you confess with your mouth Jesus as Lord, and believe in your heart that God raised Him from the dead, you will be saved; for with the heart a person believes, resulting in righteousness, and with the mouth he confesses, resulting in salvation" (Romans 10:9-10 NASB).

To be wise as a serpent, you must use the gift and the grace God has given you. You must develop the power of the mouth. You are snared with the words of your mouth and you are taken with the words of your mouth.

Thou art snared with the words of thy mouth, thou art taken with the words of thy mouth.

Proverbs 6:2

Some people are able to use their mouths as weapons more successfully than others. You can hear it in their preaching, you can hear it in their confessions, you can hear it in their counselling and you can hear it in their teaching. Become a strong proclaimer and confessor of the Word and you will be as wise as a serpent.

Seven Ways You Can Use the Power in Your Mouth

1. Develop your ability to speak forth positive confessions about your life and the ministry.

For verily I say unto you, That whosoever shall say unto this mountain, Be thou removed, and be thou cast into the sea; and shall not doubt in his heart, but shall believe that those things which he saith shall come to pass; he shall have whatsoever he saith.

Mark 11:23

2. Develop your ability to preach.

For after that in the wisdom of God the world by wisdom knew not God, it pleased God by the foolishness of preaching to save them that believe.

1 Corinthians 1:21

3. Develop your ability to teach.

And moreover, because the preacher was wise, he still taught the people knowledge; yea, he gave good heed, and sought out, and set in order many proverbs.

Ecclesiastes 12:9

4. Develop positive proclamations over your congregation.

Death and life are in the power of the tongue: and they that love it shall eat the fruit thereof.

Proverbs 18:21

5. Develop your ability to counsel and advise people.

We took sweet counsel together, and walked unto the house of God in company.

Psalm 55:14

6. **Develop your ability to bargain with men and to persuade them.**

    Knowing therefore the terror of the Lord, we persuade men; but we are made manifest unto God; and I trust also are made manifest in your consciences.

    2 Corinthians 5:11

7. **Develop your ability to create and invent with your mouth.**

    By faith we understand that the world was created by the word of God, so that what is seen was made out of things which do not appear.

    Hebrews 11:3 (RSV)

    Through faith we understand that the worlds were framed by the word of God, so that things which are seen were not made of things which do appear.

    Hebrews 11:3

CHAPTER 5

Serpents are Masters at Overcoming Handicaps

...TO HIM THAT OVERCOMETH will I give to eat of the tree of life, which is in the midst of the paradise of God.

Revelation 2:7

...TO HIM THAT OVERCOMETH will I give to eat of the hidden manna, and will give him a white stone, and in the stone a new name written, which no man knoweth saving he that receiveth it.

Revelation 2:17

TO HIM THAT OVERCOMETH will I grant to sit with me in my throne, even as I also overcame, and am set down with my Father in his throne.

Revelation 3:21

Serpents Are Wise Because
They Overcome Their Handicaps

A handicap is something that severely limits you!

A handicap is something that makes you different from others!

A handicap is a disadvantage that makes success more difficult!

A handicap is a physical or social disability that makes your participation in the ministry more difficult!

When you are as wise as a serpent, you will be able to master all your handicaps and turn them around for your good. Snakes are the most severely handicapped animals on earth because they do not have limbs. Snakes have poor eyesight, and so have heat censors that can pick up vibrations.

Snakes have no moveable eyelids. Snakes also have no external ear openings.

They are deaf and yet they are able to sense things. Snakes can pick up vibrations from the ground.

In spite of these handicaps, snakes have become the most successful predators on earth. They live and flourish where no other wild animal can live. They have worked around their handicap of not having legs and are able to go anywhere. They can climb trees, swim, and they can even fly. Snakes can move equally well on the ground, under the ground, in thick undergrowth, on trees and in water. What a wonderful success story this is! In spite of not having legs, arms or ears, snakes have been able to do what other wild animals cannot do.

Most ministers of the gospel are handicapped in one-way or the other. Remember that a handicap is a limitation that makes it more difficult to be successful. Most ministers of the gospel are limited in one area or another. Every minister of the gospel is limited by his colour, his continent, his money and his lack of resources. These handicaps or limitations present themselves to everyone. Your duty is to be as wise as a serpent and overcome your handicap. You must actually use your limitations to your advantage. The wisdom of the serpent is to refuse to succumb to the handicap you face. The wisdom of the serpent is to turn your handicap into your advantage. Serpents use the fact that they do not have legs to hide effectively. That is why a snake can live near you and you will never know. Serpents have developed special techniques for legless movement. The feared black mamba can move as fast as a hundred metre sprinter. Imagine that! The handicap of the serpent has been turned into its greatest advantage.

If you are wise as a serpent, you will not sit and moan about your lack of resources or any other handicap you have. If you are wise as a serpent, you will not allow your problems and limitations to drown your calling. You will rise up with the wisdom of a serpent and use the very handicap to your advantage.

Handicaps You Can Overcome

1. Youthfulness can be a handicap.

All through my ministry, I have been despised because I was younger than most other ministers. I used to resent being so young. I tried to grow a beard so that I would look older. I bought glasses that I would wear to make me look like an older bespectacled man. But one day, I realised that being young was actually an advantage. I began to notice how older people fell asleep helplessly during church services. I found out that there are many jobs that could only be done by young people. I found out that Old Testament priests were supposed to minister from the age of twenty-five to fifty. I became empowered when I found that young people had a great place in the work of God. That is why Paul said, "Let no man despise thy youth; but be thou an example of the believers, in word, in conversation, in charity, in spirit, in faith, in purity" (1 Timothy 4:12). Today, I am excited about being young, having young church members and preaching with a youthful style. I consider it an advantage and not a handicap.

2. Having your headquarters in Africa can be a handicap.

Africa is generally poor, disorganized and despised. Anything that is based in Africa will be affected by the poverty and the disorganisation that is prevalent there. When I began to have crusades, I felt that if my ministry were not based in Africa, I would have greater financial support to conduct crusades. I truly felt limited because I did not know any rich Americans who could give money to have a crusade. However, I began to look for the advantages with what I had. I realised that being based in Africa made me understand the terrain much better than Americans did. Being based in Africa, I was able to conduct a crusade at a fraction of the price that it would cost Americans to conduct the same crusade. A famous American evangelist saw a photograph of one of my massive crusades in Africa and said it would cost him nothing less than half a million dollars to have that crusade. I smiled to myself because it did not cost me that much. My advantage was that I was based in Africa and I knew how to get things done much more cheaply.

3. Your colour can be a handicap.

Being half African and half European has its amazing challenges. When I am in Europe and America, everyone sees me as a black man. When I am in Africa, everyone sees me as a white man. In effect, I do not belong to any of these places. I used to feel sorry for myself because of my brown colour. "I don't belong anywhere", I thought to myself. As I began to travel around the world, I found out that I actually fitted into more countries than I thought. In South Africa, I pass for a "coloured person". At different places I have been asked whether I am Somalian, Ethiopian, Malaysian, Indian, Indonesian, Pakistani, Columbian,

Brazilian, Latino, etc. As my international ministry grew, I found out that my limitation was actually an advantage.

4. Your marriage can be a handicap.

Everybody has a different kind of marriage. Some people have A1 (excellent, ideal) marriages. Others have P5 (prison, suffering, bondage) marriages. Perhaps you married someone who is not an ideal partner. Perhaps you have an unpleasant, quarrelling, malicious, and contentious wife. Perhaps you feel sad that you backed the wrong horse and are yoked to an unfortunate circumstance.

Joseph was in prison, which is a 'type' of bad marriage. He used this handicap to rise into prominence and leadership. Your difficult marriage is giving you certain important qualities. Every difficult marriage releases two key spiritual treasures into your life – humility and wisdom. People who do not have difficult marriages do not have the same level of humility as those with difficult marriages. Those who have A1 marriages often develop a subtle pride about their ideal and harmonious lives. You will hear them saying things like, "Why don't you pull yourself together and be a good husband so that you can have a good marriage?" They will suggest six principles that they have followed for years, explaining that these principles always lead to good marriages. A1 marriage partners often suffer from pride, whilst P1 marriage partners are blessed with the humility and humiliation of their circumstances.

The other key quality that is released through your difficult marriage is the key of wisdom. You need superior wisdom to outmanoeuvre a cantankerous or accusative woman and continue to dwell peacefully with her. Solomon advised dwelling in the desert or finding your way to a rooftop. It takes supernatural wisdom and strategy to dwell with an unfaithful man who beats his wife and comes home with HIV viruses to download into her.

After many years of a P5 marriage, you will become a wiser and more humble spouse who appreciates and understands other people's problems. A person with an A1 marriage will not have this advantage and can even become insensitive to people's problems.

So Joseph's master took him and put him into the jail, the place where the king's prisoners were confined; and he was there in the jail.

But the LORD was with Joseph and extended kindness to him, and gave him favor in the sight of the chief jailer.

The chief jailer committed to Joseph's charge all the prisoners who were in the jail; so that whatever was done there, he was responsible for it.

The chief jailer did not supervise anything under Joseph's charge because the LORD was with him; and whatever he did, the LORD made to prosper.

Genesis 39:20-23 (NASB)

5. Your past can be a handicap to you.

You must overcome the handicap of the sins of your past and the sins of your youth.

Remember, O LORD, Your compassion and Your lovingkindnesses, For they have been from of old.

Do not remember the sins of my youth or my transgressions; according to Your lovingkindness remember me, for Your goodness' sake, O LORD.

Psalm 25:6-7 (NASB)

Choose you this day what you prefer! Your past can become a handicap to you, or, you can manoeuvre like a serpent and turn your past life into an advantage. Your past escapades with men has become a handicap when your husband angrily mentions the footballers and boxers who have been your boyfriends. But you can turn your handicap into your advantage if you deploy the sexual skills you learnt on the "field" in your marriage. Your husband could be mesmerized by your agility and acrobatics which you learnt out there. Consider your unfortunate past as a season of training for your current marriage circumstance.

6. Being a woman can be a handicap.

Likewise, ye husbands, dwell with them according to knowledge, giving honour UNTO THE WIFE, AS UNTO THE WEAKER VESSEL, and as being heirs together of the grace of life; that your prayers be not hindered.

1 Peter 3:7

A woman is a weaker vessel. If two ships are going on a long journey, the weaker vessel will suffer more from the storms and the bad weather. The weaker vessel is likely to collapse and suffer more than the stronger ship. Women are exposed to many specific fears and temptations. Women are often mistreated and mishandled by men. But a woman can turn around her disadvantage and use it to her advantage. Women who have learnt how to do this enjoy many benefits by acting weak and vulnerable, thereby drawing the sympathy and assistance of people. Today, women have turned many laws to favour them by presenting themselves as victims of evil. This is ironic because they are equally as evil as men.

Five Principles For Overcoming Handicaps

1. **Overcome your handicaps by assuming the stance and posture of an overcomer.** Always remember that you will be rewarded for what you overcome.

2. **Overcome your handicaps by knowing that everyone has handicaps.**

   It is one of satan's deceptions to make you think you are the only one with challenges and problems.

MANY ARE THE AFFLICTIONS OF THE RIGHTEOUS: but the Lord delivereth him out of them all.

Psalm 34:19

Yea, and ALL THAT WILL LIVE GODLY IN CHRIST JESUS SHALL SUFFER persecution.

2 Timothy 3:12

3. **Overcome handicaps by thinking of a way to turn a handicap into an advantage.**

   Think of how you can turn your particular problem into an advantage for the ministry.

4. **Overcome handicaps by receiving supernatural strength for your particular handicap.**

   For this thing I besought the Lord thrice, that it might depart from me.

   And he said unto me, MY GRACE IS SUFFICIENT for thee: for MY STRENGTH IS MADE PERFECT IN WEAKNESS. Most gladly therefore will I rather glory in my infirmities, that the power of Christ may rest upon me.

   Therefore I take pleasure in infirmities, in reproaches, in necessities, in persecutions, in distresses for Christ's sake: for when I am weak, then am I strong.

   2 Corinthians 12:8-10

   There is always sufficient grace for every problem. Every problem has a solution. Every engineering problem has an engineering solution. Every problem has special grace provided for it.

5. **Overcome your handicap by embracing your God-given weaknesses. This was the secret of Apostle Paul.**

   Therefore I TAKE PLEASURE IN INFIRMITIES, in reproaches, in necessities, in persecutions, in distresses for Christ's sake: for when I am weak, then am I strong.

   2 Corinthians 12:10

29

You must overcome your handicaps by learning to take pleasure in your weaknesses. See the sometimes awkward benefits of your handicaps. Snakes can hide anywhere and move through tiny spaces. Animals with legs cannot do these things.

Accepting your weakness delivers you from wasting your energy to develop strengths you will never have.

If you are an antelope, there is no point in trying to develop the strength of your arms and legs to fight with lions. You will never have enough strength to fight a lion. If you are an antelope, there is no point in developing your teeth to be as sharp as a lion's or a crocodile's. Your weakness as an antelope is your lack of strength. But you have something else that can work for you. And that is speed and agility! Antelopes have developed their speed and agility so much that they are hardly caught by lions. The population of antelopes has increased whilst the population of lions has decreased to critically low levels.

CHAPTER 6

Masters at Giving Themselves Wholly

... give thyself wholly to them; ...

1 Timothy 4:15

Serpents Are Wise Because
They Give Themselves Wholly

A serpent is a slim long tube that moves sleekly on the ground. And yet, it is able to kill and swallow huge four-legged antelopes. It is a wonder to watch a python swallow a huge antelope together with its horns, hoofs and head. What an amazing creature that is able to overcome another animal ten times its size. What kind of wisdom is this? What kind of wisdom does a serpent use?

The wisdom of a serpent is the wisdom of giving itself wholly to its task. A serpent gives itself wholly to its vision and purpose. You should watch a snake using its whole body to kill its prey. Pythons, anacondas and boa constrictors kill their prey by constricting their prey with the entire length of their body. The snake tightens its coils around the prey to suffocate it.

Indeed, it uses its entire body to engulf its prey. Each time a captured animal takes a breath, the snake tightens its hold. The snake squeezes so tightly that its prey cannot breathe.

Snakes give themselves wholly to the killing of their prey. What has God called you to do? Pastors should give themselves wholly to the ministry. Many people do not give themselves fully to the ministry. Give yourself totally to your God-given work. Do not be impressed by ministers of the gospel who proudly tell you about the business they do on the side. You must have a special calling to be involved in para-business hybrid ministries! The Bible tells us to give ourselves wholly to the ministry. If you give yourself wholly to the ministry, you will see a great difference in your life.

Perhaps, if you were to give yourself wholly to ministry, you would become more anointed and help many more people. Perhaps if you were to give yourself wholly to the ministry, many more people would be saved. Your hybrid ministry is not yielding the results that it should. Paul did not encourage para-business ministry hybrids. He said you should give yourself wholly to the ministry and to the call of God.

Jesus gave himself fully to the ministry and bore much fruit. Our Lord Jesus was a carpenter. At a point, He laid aside carpentry, and went fully into preaching, teaching and healing. What would have happened to us if He had continued to build a para-carpentry hybrid ministry? Where did we learn to develop these hybrid ministries? "Have this attitude in yourselves which was also in Christ Jesus…" (Philippians 2:5 NASB)

Peter gave himself fully to the ministry and bore much fruit. Peter was a fisherman. But a time came when he had to stop fishing and follow the Lord. That was full time ministry. Peter said, "Behold, we have left everything and followed You" (Mark 10:28).

Paul gave himself fully to the ministry and bore much fruit. Paul was also a tent maker. But a time came when he gave himself wholly to the Lord and the benefits were seen by all. He considered every other thing, apart from the call of God, as pure rubbish. "More than that, I count all things to be loss in view of the surpassing value of knowing Christ Jesus my Lord, for whom I have suffered the loss of all things, and count them but rubbish so that I may gain Christ" (Philippians 3:8 NASB).

How To Give Yourself Wholly

To give yourself wholly to the ministry is to throw in everything that you possess. Throw everything that you have control of into the ministry. When you give yourself wholly, you will not have any time or strength to do other things. There are fifteen different things that you must give in order to say that you have given yourself wholly. Every single one of these components makes a difference to your life and ministry. Your level of fruitfulness changes when you give each one of these items.

1. *To give yourself wholly is to give your heart to the Lord.* People who give themselves to the ministry but do not give their hearts are just miming and acting. God is not interested in actors. He wants people who are serving Him from the heart.

2. *To give yourself wholly is to give your intelligence.* Were you good at school? Did you do well in Maths, Physics, Biology, Chemistry or Statistics? God can use your intelligence and it will make a big difference to the ministry. Look around and you will see that ministries, which also use their minds and intelligence, last much longer than those who don't.

3. *To give yourself wholly is to give your temperament.* Are you a choleric or a melancholic person? Use it for the church. I have used my personality to develop the church into a worldwide and structured denomination. The melancholic part of my temperament has helped me to structure a complicated network of churches. The choleric aspect of my temperament has helped me to work with speed and to take decisions that are necessary for true advancement.

4. *To give yourself wholly is to give your ideas.* An idea can make the difference to your entire ministry. Everyone receives heavenly ideas that are actually words of wisdom. These ideas float into your mind when you are relaxed. Instead of deploying these ideas to make a bank prosper or a petrol station make more sales, you must use these God-given ideas to make the church advance.

5. *To give yourself wholly is to give your education.* Are you educated? You must have learnt something in school. I am sad to say that most people do not apply the things they learnt in school in their daily lives. I learnt many things in secondary school and also in the university. I am constantly using these things to develop the ministry and to build the church. Pastors and ministers must not send their minds on a vacation just because they are in the ministry. Use everything you have and be as wise as a serpent.

6. *To give yourself wholly is to give your connections.* Whom do you know? You must know somebody important. Use that connection for the church. Have you noticed how businessmen are constantly seeking to use their connections

to make more money? To give yourself wholly is to use all the connections you have to help the church to work.

7. *To give yourself wholly is to give your gifts.* Your gift is the thing you are able to do which others find very difficult to do.

8. *To give yourself wholly is to give your skills.* There are certain skills you have acquired as you grow up. I can play the piano, the drums and guitar. I have used these skills to develop the church and the music ministry. What skills do you have?

9. *To give yourself wholly is to give your background.* Use whatever background you have. I have a pastor who used to be a hunter. He would hunt fearlessly in the deep and dark forest in the middle of the night. He slept peacefully on the leaves in the forest anytime he was tired. It is against this background that he felt the call of God and became a minister of the gospel. I also have a pastor who used to be a fisherman, fishing for shrimps in the deep ocean in between Ghana and Cote d'Ivoire in the middle of the night.

Your background will definitely have a part to play in your calling. Give everything to God. There is no need to run a hybrid ministry. You can give yourself wholly to what you believe in.

10. *To give yourself wholly is to give your time.* You must give your morning, evening and noontime to the Lord. Any minister who has enough time to do other things must realise that what you give to business is what you could have given to the Lord. I was running a business when the Lord asked me to give myself wholly to the ministry. I then gave up my hybrid ministry and all the time that I would have spent following my truck around, I spent serving the Lord.

11. *To give yourself wholly is to give your family.* Give your wife and give your children to the Lord. It is a wonder that

many ministers of the gospel do not want their children to serve in the ministry. There is no higher job and no better place for your family to be than in the ministry. When your family joins you in the ministry, your ministry will go higher.

12. *To give yourself wholly is to give your home.* Give your home to the ministry by making it a centre of hospitality and refreshment.

13. *To give yourself wholly is to give your money.* One of the ways to check if your heart is right is to give your money also. Many ministers expect people to give money, but they must also put their money into the ministry.

14. To give yourself wholly is to give your assets. What do you own? Throw it in and God will bless you. I once received a gift of beautiful desks and cabinets. Our church office did not have such desks. I immediately gave everything to the church office. Our ministry office was transformed overnight with this contribution. I had given myself, I had given my time, but I was also giving my assets.

15. *To give yourself wholly is to give your energy.* I am constantly amazed at people who have no energy for the church. Yet they have energy to stay up watching films for hours on end. Indeed, energy is released for everything else but God! Throw in your energy as well. Give your energy to God. Get tired doing the work of God, giving Him the best days of your life.

CHAPTER 7

Masters of Manoeuvres

But what think ye? A certain man had two sons; and he came to the first, and said, Son, go work to day in my vineyard. He answered and said, I will not: but AFTERWARD HE REPENTED, and went. And he came to the second, and said likewise. And he answered and said, I go, sir: and went not.

Matthew 21:28-30

The Serpent is Wise Because of its Manoeuverability

S nakes are the masters of many manoeuvres! They can move in many different ways. Serpents can climb, they can swim, they can stand, they can move forward, they can move sideways and they can even move backwards.

A snake can contour its body to ride in the air like the wing of an aeroplane and can even steer its body to a particular landing spot. Flying snakes glide in the air and are able to glide to a distance of 100m.

All snakes can swim quite well. Most snakes can climb trees. rat snakes and pythons are excellent examples of good climbers. The skull of a snake is a highly evolved complex structure that is characterised by mobility and flexibility. Snakes have a greatly reduced weight of the skull that allows greater mobility of the skull.

Most of the bones within the snake skull are not fused, but rather loosely attached by ligaments. This allows the expansion and flexion necessary to engulf prey. In addition to the reduced number of bones within the skull there are also several hinge joints located at various points that allow the movement and slight rotation of certain segments. This enhanced flexibility of a serpent allows it to manoeuvre its way out of tight spots and into tiny corners.

Flexibility and manoeuvrability are important for success. All huge organisations are in danger of becoming so stiff that they cannot change and move around. Without manoeuvrability, you lose the ability to quickly respond to the ever-changing scenes of life. Do you know that nothing is ever going to remain the same? What allowed for success five years ago is not likely to work in the same way today.

Building a church today is a little different from building a church a decade ago. You have to use different strategies and different keys. Conducting a crusade some years ago is different from conducting a crusade today. This is because the nature of the population has even changed. Many African cities are filled with aggressive people seeking their fortunes. This is not how these cities were some years ago. Many people have come from the hinterland, having been abandoned by the governments of the day. This has also caused an influx of people with other religions. Your inability to manoeuvre and to change will spell your downfall.

There are some things that never change. Prayer and the truths of the word of God are unchanging but the way we minister these things will change. The snake is a very wise creature because it does not maintain one form or shape. It can undergo every kind of manoeuvre to get in or out of a place. Can you undergo a major change in your presentation? Can you make a U-turn, a right turn or a left turn right now? To be as wise as a serpent you must be capable of such manoeuvres.

1. To be wise as a serpent you must be capable of 'U'-turns.

I WILL ARISE and go to my father, and will say unto him, Father, I have sinned against heaven, and before thee, and am no more worthy to be called thy son: make me as one of thy hired servants.

AND HE AROSE, and came to his father. But when he was yet a great way off, his father saw him, and had compassion, and ran, and fell on his neck, and kissed him.

Luke 15:18-20

The prodigal son gives us the best example of a 'U'-turn.

A 'U'-turn is a reversal of your former decisions. He reversed all his former decisions and humbly returned to his proper place. That is what I call a spiritual 'U'-turn. A spiritual 'U'-turn is a manoeuvre in which you reverse and go back on decisions you have made earlier. If you are not capable of 'U'-turns, you are not capable of repenting from your mistakes.

Zacchaeus made a 'U'-turn when he met Jesus Christ.

He turned away from corruption and swindling people. A 'U'-turn is true repentance.

And Zacchaeus stood, and said unto the Lord; Behold, Lord, the half of my goods I give to the poor; and if I have taken any thing from any man by false accusation, I restore him fourfold.

Luke 19:8

We all make many mistakes and when you realise that you have made a mistake you must be able to make a U-turn. I came to realise the importance of those things and that is why I made a U-turn. After our church began, I realised I had made a mistake in the way our church started. I made a U-turn and went back to apologise.

How old are you? How is it that you cannot say sorry for what you have done? How come you are inflexible and unchangeable? Your inflexibility can cost you your life! Make yourself malleable and flexible in the hands of the Holy Spirit.

There are many things I said I would not do that I do today. I said I did not need a secretary but today I have several secretaries. I said my assistant would be an evangelist whilst I would be a pastor. But I made a U-turn when I realised the Lord wanted me to have crusades. If I did not practice spiritual U-turns, I would not have begun Healing Jesus Crusades. I said I would drive certain cars when I became fifty years old, because no one would criticise me then. When I was twenty-five years old, I thought a fifty-year old man was a very old man. But when I became fifty years old I refused to own any such car. I realised that I had underestimated how quickly I would become fifty years old.

2. To be as wise as a serpent you must be capable of a C-turn.

Jesus was capable of a 'C'-turn.

Serpents are capable of C-turns. A C-turn is a swerve to the side. It is not a reversal but it is a manoeuvre that takes you off the wrong course onto a better way. Jesus made a C-turn and moved away from the country of the Gadarenes when the people desired Him to leave.

> And all the people of the country of the Gerasenes and the surrounding district asked him to leave them, for they were gripped with great fear; and he got into a boat and returned.
>
> Luke 8:37 (NASB)

Jesus did not stop His ministry of casting out devils and healing people. He just shifted from the country of the Gadarenes to where He was more welcome. It is not wisdom to be too stiff or insistent on your original plan. That can get you into big trouble. You must be flexible and capable of C-turns.

Peter was capable of a 'C'-turn.

Peter had dedicated his life to fishing. Some of you have dedicated your lives to practicing medicine, law, pharmacy, carpentry and computer science. Are you not capable of a C-turn? Peter, the fisherman became Peter the apostle because he was capable of swerving off the layman's road and into full time ministry. What makes you so rigid? How old are you? How come you are inflexible and unchangeable? Inflexibility can be dangerous when it comes to following God.

> Now as Jesus was walking by the Sea of Galilee, He saw two brothers, Simon who was called Peter, and Andrew his brother, casting a net into the sea; for they were fishermen. And He said to them, "Follow Me, and I will make you fishers of men." IMMEDIATELY THEY LEFT THEIR NETS and followed Him.
>
> Matthew 4:18-20 (NASB)

Andrew and John were capable of a 'C'-turn.

These two men were disciples and followers of John the Baptist. Actually, they were disciples who were seeking the Lord. When John pointed out the Lamb of God they knew it was time to move on. They did not make a U-turn away from the ministry. They made a C-turn which took them deeper and further into God. The C-turn they took brought them closer to Jesus.

> Again the next day John was standing with two of his disciples, and he looked at Jesus as He walked, and said, "Behold, the Lamb of God!" The two disciples heard him speak, and THEY FOLLOWED JESUS.
>
> John 1:35-37 (NASB)

3. To be as wise a serpent you must be capable of stopping.

> As Jesus was approaching Jericho, a blind man was sitting by the road begging.
>
> Now hearing a crowd going by, he began to inquire what this was. They told him that Jesus of Nazareth was passing by.
>
> And he called out, saying, "Jesus, Son of David, have mercy on me!"
>
> Those who led the way were sternly telling him to be quiet; but he kept crying out all the more, "Son of David, have mercy on me!"
>
> AND JESUS STOPPED and commanded that he be brought to Him; and when he came near, He questioned him, "What do you want Me to do for you?" And he said, "Lord, I want to regain my sight!"
>
> And Jesus said to him, "Receive your sight; your faith has made you well."
>
> Immediately he regained his sight and began following Him, glorifying God; and when all the people saw it, they gave praise to God.
>
> Luke 18:35-43 (NASB)

Jesus was capable of stopping.

As Jesus approached Jericho, He heard a cry which stopped Him in his tracks. It was blind Bartimaeus who stopped Jesus

Christ on His journey to Jerusalem. Jesus Christ was capable of stopping even though He was already in motion. A good minister must be able to stop dead in his tracks. You must be able to stop what you are doing even though you are already in motion. There are crusades that we had prepared for that we simply stopped. Why not? You must be able to stop! A good car must be able to stop anywhere! A good minister must be able to stop preaching after twenty minutes if that is what is required of you. It cannot be that you can only preach for one hour.

God is teaching you how to manoeuvre. To be as wise as a serpent, you must be flexible, ready to go for days but also be ready to stop dead in your tracks. Balaam the prophet was unable to stop going in the wrong direction even though the angel warned him. That is a very dangerous thing. In the end, the donkey was forced to speak to the prophet.

> And God's anger was kindled because he went: and the angel of the LORD stood in the way for an adversary against him. Now he was riding upon his ass, and his two servants were with him. And the ass saw the angel of the LORD standing in the way, and his sword drawn in his hand: and the ass turned aside out of the way, and went into the field: and Balaam smote the ass, to turn her into the way.
>
> But the angel of the LORD stood in a path of the vineyards, a wall being on this side, and a wall on that side.
>
> And when the ass saw the angel of the LORD, she thrust herself unto the wall, and crushed Balaam's foot against the wall: and he smote her again.
>
> And the angel of the LORD went further, and stood in a narrow place, where was no way to turn either to the right hand or to the left.
>
> And when the ass saw the angel of the LORD, she fell down under Balaam: and Balaam's anger was kindled, and he smote the ass with a staff.

43

And the LORD opened the mouth of the ass, and she said unto Balaam, What have I done unto thee, that thou hast smitten me these three times?

And Balaam said unto the ass, Because thou hast mocked me: I would there were a sword in mine hand, for now would I kill thee.

And the ass said unto Balaam, Am not I thine ass, upon which thou hast ridden ever since I was thine unto this day? was I ever wont to do so unto thee? And he said, Nay.

Then the LORD opened the eyes of Balaam, and he saw the angel of the LORD standing in the way, and his sword drawn in his hand: and he bowed down his head, and fell flat on his face.

And the angel of the LORD said unto him, Wherefore hast thou smitten thine ass these three times? behold, I went out to withstand thee, because thy way is perverse before me:

And the ass saw me, and turned from me these three times: unless she had turned from me, surely now also I had slain thee, and saved her alive.

Numbers 22:22-33

4. To be as wise as a serpent you must be capable of moving out.

The disciples were given the explicit command to go into the world and preach the gospel, but they did not go because they had become happy and established in Jerusalem. They were stuck in the mud! This is a dangerous phenomenon and it is happening in the church today. You must be capable of moving out of comfortable and cozy cities into the fields which are ripe unto harvest. There can be no clearer command than this: "GO YE therefore, and teach all nations, baptizing them in the name of the Father, and of the Son, and of the Holy Ghost" (Matthew 28:19).

But look how long it took them to get going. From Matthew 28, it took eight long chapters in the book of Acts before they were dislodged from Jerusalem. They simply could not go because of the revival, the joy, the miracles and the church growth they were experiencing in Jerusalem.

If you will not go with the command, you will be moved by troubles, tribulations and difficulties. Read it for yourself: "... And at that time there was a GREAT PERSECUTION against the church which was at Jerusalem; and THEY WERE ALL SCATTERED abroad throughout the regions of Judaea and Samaria, except the apostles....Therefore they that were scattered abroad went everywhere preaching the word" (Acts 8:1,4).

5. To be as wise as a serpent you must be able to stop and start again.

Jesus Christ was as wise as a serpent. He was able to start, He was able to stop and start again! He said He would not go up to the feast. A few days later, He changed his mind and said, "I'm going up." He went up, and this time, He went up secretly. Why are you so rigid when your Saviour was able to stop and start again? What have you stopped that you need to start again? Remember the man whom Jesus recommended. "A certain man had two sons; and he came to the first, and said, Son, go work to day in my vineyard. he answered and said, I will not: but afterward he repented, and went" (Matthew 21:28-29). That is the spirit of wisdom. You can stop, but you can start again.

> Go ye up unto this feast: I GO NOT up yet unto this feast; for my time is not yet full come. When he had said these words unto them, he abode still in Galilee. But when his brethren were gone up, THEN WENT HE also up unto the feast, not openly, but as it were in secret.
>
> John 7:8-10

CHAPTER 8

Masters of Survival

I know both how to be abased, and I know how to abound: EVERY WHERE AND IN ALL THINGS I AM INSTRUCTED BOTH TO BE FULL AND TO BE HUNGRY, both to abound and to suffer need.

Philippians 4:12

Serpents Are Wise Because
They Can Survive Anywhere

To survive means to endure and to remain in existence in spite of all circumstances. It also means to get along and remain healthy, happy and unaffected in spite of the circumstances. Most of us are quenched by unhappy events and circumstances but a survivor continues to exist after adversity or hardship.

Snakes are by far the most successful survivors in the world. They have survived in all kinds of environments. Compare this with other animals. For instance, there are no more lions in Ghana and in many other countries. Snakes on the other hand abound in Ghana.

Most of us can only live in one kind of environment. The gospel is not being spread today because even Africans who grew up in villages claim they can only live in America and therefore cannot be sent into the world. The polar bear is different from a snake because it can only live in a very cold environment. On the other hand, there are 2,700 species of snake in the world of all colours and sizes that can live virtually anywhere.

Serpents are so wise that they can live at ground level or in trees. Serpents can live underground or even in the sea. There are snakes that live 16,000 feet up in the Himalayas. Some live in the scorching waterless deserts. Some live as far north as the Arctic Circle and many inhabit tropical forests. There are only a few places that do not have snakes.

These survivors come in all sizes; very small and very large. That is one of the secrets of surviving: you must come in all sizes. We must have both big and small churches if the ministry is to persist through the changing scenes of life. The smallest snake lives in buildings - in any town or city and anywhere. It can be transported in the soil of plants to garden centres all over the world. At the other end of the scale, the world's largest snake and the heaviest snake is the anaconda. It can reach nearly 9 metres in length. It has a bodily girth of a pig and weighs about 200 kilograms.

When you are as wise as a serpent, there is nowhere God cannot send you. Ministers of the gospel are no longer as wise as serpents. Perhaps we can say that they are as wise as a polar bear that means they can only stay in one environment.

A minister must not flourish only in 'good' circumstances. He must do well whatever the circumstances. Joseph did well as a slave and in the slave environment. "Now Joseph had been taken down to Egypt; and Potiphar, an Egyptian officer of Pharaoh, the captain of the bodyguard, bought him from the Ishmaelites, who had taken him down there. The LORD was with Joseph, so he became a successful man. And he was in the house of his master, the Egyptian. Now his master saw that the LORD was with him and how the LORD caused all that he did to prosper in his hand. So Joseph found favor in his sight and became his personal servant; and he made him overseer over his house, and all that he owned he put in his charge" (Genesis 39:1-4 NASB).

He did well as a prisoner and in the prison cell environment. In both situations he excelled so much that he was put in charge. Joseph was a survivor. "So Joseph's master took him and put him into the jail, the place where the king's prisoners were confined; and he was there in the jail. But the LORD was with Joseph and extended kindness to him, and gave him favor in the sight of the chief jailer. The chief jailer committed to Joseph's charge all the prisoners who were in the jail; so that whatever was done there, he was responsible for it. The chief jailer did not supervise anything under Joseph's charge because the LORD was with him; and whatever he did, the LORD made to prosper" (Genesis 39:20-23).

One day, I was discussing my troubles with a fellow minister of the gospel. He was a senior minister and a father of many ministers. I told him how I had been harassed by the government. I explained how a government agency had summoned me for investigations and interrogation and had made me fill so many forms about my personal life.

To my amazement, he laughed and congratulated me. "Congratulations for what" I thought. 'My troubles?'

He explained, "Ministry is not about how big your church is or what car you drive."

He continued, "It is about "what have you survived! What have you been through?"

He said, "Ministry is about 'What have you suffered?"

Then he told me, "I have been harassed by these same people five times. I have filled those same forms that you filled five times."

I was stunned. I never imagined that he had been through all that.

A true minister is a survivor. In spite of the circumstances and environment, he survives and prevails. Paul was a survivor. He described the circumstances he had encountered. Just like this senior minister I spoke to, the apostle Paul seemed almost nostalgic about the troubles he had survived.

Stop giving excuses and become a survivor of different circumstances!

Can You Survive what Paul Survived?

1. You must survive and minister the gospel in spite of restrictions or imprisonment.

Are they ministers of Christ? (I speak as a fool) I am more; in labours more abundant, in stripes above measure, IN PRISONS more frequent, in deaths oft.

2 Corinthians 11:23

Fear none of those things which thou shalt suffer: behold, the devil shall cast some of you into prison, that ye may be tried; and ye shall have tribulation ten days: be thou faithful unto death, and I will give thee a crown of life. He that hath an ear, let him hear what the Spirit saith unto the churches; He that overcometh shall not be hurt of the second death.

Revelation 2:10-11

2. You must survive and minister the gospel in spite of accidents, near-death experiences and their aftermath.

....IN DEATHS OFT ...Thrice was I beaten with rods, once was I stoned, thrice I SUFFERED SHIPWRECK, a night and a day I have been in the deep;

2 Corinthians 11:23,25

3. You must survive and minister the gospel in spite of the dangers of your city.

...IN PERILS IN THE CITY, in perils in the wilderness, in perils in the sea, in perils among false brethren;

2 Corinthians 11:26

4. You must survive and minister the gospel in spite of the danger of armed robbers.

In journeyings often, in perils of waters, in PERILS OF ROBBERS, in perils by mine own countrymen, in perils by the heathen, in perils in the city, in perils in the wilderness, in perils in the sea, in perils among false brethren;

2 Corinthians 11:26

5. You must survive and minister the gospel in spite of hunger.

In weariness and painfulness, in watchings often, IN HUNGER and thirst, in fastings often, in cold and nakedness.

2 Corinthians 11: 27

6. You must survive and minister the gospel in spite of under-development and the wilderness circumstances of your country.

In journeyings often, in perils of waters, in perils of robbers, in perils by mine own countrymen, in perils by the heathen, in perils in the city, in perils in the WILDERNESS, in perils in the sea, in perils among false brethren;

2 Corinthians 11:26

7. You must survive and minister the gospel in spite of disloyalty and false brethren.

In journeyings often, in perils of waters, in perils of robbers, in perils by mine own countrymen, in perils by the heathen, in perils in the city, in perils in the wilderness, in perils in the sea, in perils among FALSE BRETHREN;

2 Corinthians 11:26

8. You must survive and minister the gospel in spite of your tiredness.

IN WEARINESS and painfulness, in watchings often, in hunger and thirst, in fastings often, in cold and nakedness.

2 Corinthians 11: 27

9. You must survive and minister the gospel in spite of your lack of sleep.

In weariness and painfulness, IN WATCHINGS often, in hunger and thirst, in fastings often, in cold and nakedness.

2 Corinthians 11: 27

10. You must survive and minister the gospel in spite of the weather.

In weariness and painfulness, in watchings often, in hunger and thirst, in fastings often, IN COLD and nakedness.

2 Corinthians 11: 27

CHAPTER 9

Masters of Contentment

... for I have learned, in whatsoever state I am, therewith to be content.

Philippians 4:11

Serpents Are Wise Because They Are Content With Very Little

T oday, most of us do not live with the wisdom of the serpent who is content with very little. When I saw a snake in the sands of the desert, I wondered what the snake would eat and how it would be able to survive in the Sahara Desert. Amazingly, the serpent is able to stay in the dry arid Sahara desert as well as in the cold icy snow of the Artic Circle. The first question that comes to mind is "What food will the snake eat?"

Some snakes can eat once a year or once every few months. How many of us can do that? Not having to eat very often is one of the keys to the success of snakes everywhere.

Snakes are masters of contentment because with very little, they are able to live for many years. They eat once a while. Snakes don't have to eat often and need a twentieth of the food of warm-blooded mammals their size. Because they have a slow metabolic rate, they can survive without eating for many days at a stretch. After a big meal, a king cobra can survive for many months without food.

When a minister of the gospel has the wisdom of a serpent, he will be able to live without needing many things. Like snakes, ministers must not need many things for the ministry to do well.

If you are wise as a serpent, you will not need to have an air-conditioned house, a special car, a special house, a special office, etc., in order to work for the Lord.

Do not be deceived into thinking that the world has been reached with the gospel. Television ministry is not a substitute for a real pastor who lives in the village where the people need him. But where are the pastors who will go to the towns, the villages and the highways? The people who would have gone on these missions are prosperity-seeking members of large churches all over the world. To send such people, you would need to provide a certain kind of house, electricity, generators, special jeeps, special communication gadgets, a personal air ambulance service, emergency stand-by doctors, international schools for their children, and the list goes on.

The serpent, however, does not need all these things to survive. It actually needs very little to stay alive and to persist in that environment. Today, there are many countries that do not have electricity and water at all. Some of these places are in great need of pastors and evangelists. Who will go there? Only those with the wisdom of the serpent! Only those with the wisdom of contentment!

The Spirit of Discontentment

I have seen all the works that are done under the sun; and, behold, all is vanity and VEXATION of spirit.

Ecclesiastes 1:14

The works that are done under the sun are the works of the world. They all yield vanities and vexation of spirit. The word vexation is a Hebrew word 'reut' which means *grasping*, *longing* and *striving*. Can't you see that our lives are filled with searchings, graspings, strivings for things we will never attain? Everybody wants a bigger house, more money, more land, more cars, more women, more men and more love.

Listen to me: You either have the spirit of contentment or the spirit of the world! When you have the spirit of the world, you are full of grasping desires for what everyone else has. How can you be content when you are filled with grasping, longing and striving for the things in this world? If you see someone with something you must also have it. It is this spirit of comparison and competitiveness that opens the door for the demons of the world to flood into your soul. The spirit of the world is described clearly in the bible. "For all that is in the world, the lust of the flesh, and the lust of the eyes, and the pride of life, is not of the Father, but is of the world" (1 John 2:16).

How can you work for the Lord when you are following the burning desires of your eyes and your flesh?

Discontentment is what caused the kings of Israel to fall into error. God warned them not to go grasping after many extra things. Similarly, God is warning pastors and ministers of the gospel not to seek to multiply worldly things unto our lives.

But HE SHALL NOT MULTIPLY HORSES TO HIMSELF, nor cause the people to return to Egypt, to the end that he should multiply horses: forasmuch as the Lord hath said unto you, Ye shall henceforth return no more that way.

NEITHER SHALL HE MULTIPLY WIVES TO HIMSELF, that his heart turn not away: NEITHER SHALL HE GREATLY MULTIPLY TO HIMSELF SILVER AND GOLD.

Deuteronomy 17:14-17

When you have the spirit of contentment, the desire for all these things goes and your love is turned towards the Lord. Then you set your affection on things above and desire the will of God and the presence of God more than anything else. With the spirit of contentment, you are then happy to get along with whatever basic things are available.

Paul and the Spirit of Contentment

Paul had the spirit of contentment. He had received a command from the Lord to be content in every circumstance. To be content means to be stable, happy and satisfied with your circumstances. God's command to us is to have a spirit of contentment. Paul reveals that God had instructed him to have that attitude. Amazingly, Christians today do not have that attitude. Is it that we are not hearing the voice of God? Has the spirit of the world taken over?

Not that I speak in respect of want: for I have learned, in whatsoever state I am, therewith to be content. I know both how to be abased, and I know how to abound: every where and in all things I AM INSTRUCTED both to be full and to be hungry, both to abound and to suffer need. I can do all things through Christ which strengtheneth me.

Philippians 4:11-13

Discontentment Can Make You Lose Everything

1. **Discontentment is dangerous because it makes you reach out for things God has withheld from you.** Do you know that God withholds certain things from you? God may have withheld riches from you but given you a faithful husband. He may have withheld an international ministry from you but given you a great national ministry. There is always something you do not have and you must be careful when you go out seeking for things you do not have. You don't have to add to the list of discontented people below.

   a. Adam was given ten thousand million trees but God withheld the tree of the knowledge of good and evil. He reached out for the tree of the knowledge of good and evil and he lost his place in the Garden of Eden.

   b. Ahab was given Israel but he was not given Naboth's vineyard. He reached out for Naboth's vineyard and he lost his kingship.

   c. David was given lots of women but was not given Bathsheba. He reached out to take Bathsheba and he lost his peace.

   d. Absalom was given the right to be a prince and an important person but was not given the kingdom. He reached out for the kingdom and lost his life.

   e. Gehazi was given the privilege of becoming Elisha's successor. He reached out to get some money and clothes and lost his ministry.

   Discontentment is an open door for satan to tempt you. God has chosen to give you certain things and has also chosen to withhold certain things from you. "For the LORD Most High is to be feared, a great King over all the earth. He subdues peoples under us and nations under our feet. HE CHOOSES OUR INHERITANCE FOR US..." (Psalm 47:2-4 NASB).

Roots of Discontentment : Comparison and Jealousy

Comparison and jealousy are the roots of discontentment. You are comparing yourself with the wrong thing. Through comparison you will give yourself a wrong vision for your life. God has a special calling for you that does not compare with anyone else. Why are you comparing yourself with the wrong people? Why are you becoming jealous? You are opening the door for the spirit of discontentment and destruction. Whenever snakes step out of their hiding places to seek for food, they endanger their lives. When the snake sleeps in its hiding place without seeking for more food it is often safe.

1. **Comparison is a root of discontentment.** When you are discontent you start to compare. Comparison is dangerous because you often come to the wrong conclusion.

   For WE DARE NOT make ourselves of the number, or COMPARE OURSELVES with some that commend themselves: but they measuring themselves by themselves, and comparing themselves among themselves, are not wise.

   2 Corinthians 10:12

2. **Jealousy is a root of discontentment.** Instead of being happy with what God has given you, you look over your shoulder to see what God has given someone else. We are often happier until we know what someone else has. The labourers in the story below were very happy with their wages until they found out what others were receiving. That knowledge sparked off their discontentment. This is why salaries, wages and benefits are sometimes kept secret to avoid the stirring up of discontentment and ill-will.

And when they had received it, they murmured against the goodman of the house, Saying, These last have wrought but one hour, and THOU HAST MADE THEM EQUAL UNTO US, which have borne the burden and heat of the day. But he answered one of them, and said, Friend, I do thee no wrong: didst not thou agree with me for a penny? Take that thine is, and go thy way: I will give unto this last, even as unto thee. Is it not lawful for me to do what I will with mine own? Is thine eye evil, because I am good?

Matthew 20:11-15

CHAPTER 10

Masters of Patience

I waited patiently for the Lord; and he inclined unto me, and heard my cry.

Psalm 40:1

Serpents Are Wise Because
They Are Patient

Patiently waiting is one of the secrets of a serpent and must be one of the secrets of all pastors. A snake will lie patiently in wait for its prey. Snakes are masters of patience and masters of ambush. Just as the snake obtains food through patience, a minister will get what he needs through patience. We talk about the patience of Job but we must be respectful of the patience of a snake.

Snakes lie in wait patiently. Sometimes, they lie in water, waiting for the prey to come by for a drink. If you patiently observe the surface of a pond, you may see the head of a snake rising partially to the surface to take a breath every few minutes. The hours pass. Animals come and go.

Night comes, day comes and still the serpent waits patiently. Days pass! The vibration of feet and silhouettes of animals are detected by the patient serpent. Finally, it chooses its prey and strikes when least expected!

The serpent will not eat if it is not patient. Neither will you have many of the things God has ordained for you without patience. To be as wise as a serpent you must learn to be as patient as a serpent!

What You Cannot Do Without Patience

1. **You cannot have victory over your enemies if you do not learn to wait patiently for the Lord.** Learn to sit down and wait for the Lord to act. We must wait until the Lord makes the move.

   The LORD said unto my Lord, SIT THOU at my right hand, UNTIL I MAKE thine enemies thy footstool. The LORD shall send the rod of thy strength out of Zion: rule thou in the midst of thine enemies.

   Psalm 110:1-2

2. **You cannot be a godly person if you are not patient because God is a God of patience.** Impatience is a sign of ungodliness.

   Now THE GOD OF PATIENCE and consolation grant you to be likeminded one toward another according to Christ Jesus:

   Romans 15:5

3. **You cannot finish your calling if you are not patient.** Your calling needs patient work adding block by block until the whole house is built.

   Wherefore seeing we also are compassed about with so great a cloud of witnesses, let us lay aside every weight, and the sin which doth so easily beset us, and LET US RUN WITH PATIENCE the race that is set before us,

   Hebrews 12:1

4. **You cannot reap your harvest and receive your rewards without patience.** Many people give up just before the reward is due.

   And let us not be weary in well doing: for in due season we shall reap, if we faint not.

   Galatians 6:9

5. **You cannot become a man of experience without patience.** A minister must allow trials and tribulation to produce patience in him.

   And not only so, but we glory in tribulations also: knowing that TRIBULATION WORKETH PATIENCE; and PATIENCE, EXPERIENCE; and experience, hope: And hope maketh not ashamed; because the love of God is shed abroad in our hearts by the Holy Ghost which is given unto us.

   Romans 5:3-5

6. **You cannot be a perfect minister of the gospel without patience.** Through patience, you will be perfect and entire, wanting nothing.

   My brethren, count it all joy when ye fall into divers temptations; knowing this, that the trying of your faith worketh patience. But LET PATIENCE HAVE HER PERFECT WORK, THAT YE MAY BE PERFECT and entire, wanting nothing.

   James 1:2-4

CHAPTER 11

Masters of Frugality

He also that is slothful in his work is brother to him that is a great waster.

Proverbs 18:9

Serpents Are Wise Because
They Do Not Waste Anything

Serpents are masters of frugality. They do not waste anything – when they eat an animal they eat the flesh, the horns, the bones! Snakes digest everything! Nothing goes to waste. Have you ever wondered what happens when a snake swallows an antelope? Where do the horns, flesh, hoofs, hair and teeth go? Snakes waste nothing and that is why they are the most successful predators on this earth. Poor countries are usually run by great wasters. Rich countries are usually run by frugal leaders who leave nothing to waste. "There is treasure to be desired and oil in the dwelling of the wise; but a foolish man spendeth it up" (Proverbs 21:20). This is why rich people stop having pity on poor people because many poor people are great wasters.

Seven Discoveries in a Poor country

1. I discovered a poor country that was suffering from a lack of water. Most areas in the capital city did not have running water. Amazingly, the capital city of that country had huge lakes on the outskirts of the city which were used to pump fresh water into the city. Can you believe that sixty per cent of the water pumped went to waste through burst pipes and unchecked leakage?

2. I discovered a poor country which had embassies all over the world. This poor country could not build its own roads and even toilets. Yet, it maintained embassies that cost thousands and thousands of dollars to run every month. I visited some of the embassies of this poor country and it would have a staff of ten to twenty-five well-educated people who have almost nothing to do. Instead of building an embassy, they had rented expensive buildings in the capital city for decades. Can you imagine the cost of a highly indebted and poor African country running fully staffed embassies in Tokyo, New York, Geneva, Brussels,

Copenhagen, Paris, Berlin, Rome, The Hague, Moscow, Madrid, Beijing, Kuala Lumpur, Ottawa and so on. Fantastic! Poor people are usually great wasters.

3. I discovered a poor country that was suffering from lack of food, lack of employment and a lack of everything. This poor country had to import millions of dollars of rice, meat and sugar. I decided to take a drive through that country. Did I see well-cultivated farms? No. I saw miles and miles of uncultivated bushes. You would have thought that every square inch of that poor nation would be used for farming so that they would not need to import food.

4. I discovered a poor country with high unemployment rates. Yet, this country sidelined half of the population because they did not vote for them. All the brains and good leaders who could help the nation were set aside, unused and wasted. Instead of the young people being mobilized to build roads and railways, citizens of other countries were brought in to develop the nation. I also saw how a few rich men and businessmen were hounded out of the country and prevented from doing their businesses because they belonged to the wrong political party.

5. I discovered a poor country that was suffering from chronic power outages. This country could not generate enough electricity to supply its needs. The lights would go on and off at random. Yet, thousands of lights and air conditioners were left on endlessly, day and night in most of the government offices. So much of the electricity in this poor country was wasted. Another sad feature was that this country had a lot of rivers that could be dammed. Yet, all the rivers were left to run freely into the sea, wasting a valuable source of hydro-electric power. This nation even developed a nickname for its on-and-off power supply.

6. I discovered a poor country that was blessed with miles and miles of a beautiful ocean shoreline. These beaches could have attracted thousands of tourists every year. Can you

believe that the beaches in this country are rather used as toilets? Also, the miles and miles of salty sea water could have been used to generate tons of salt. Sadly, very little salt is generated by this country.

7. I discovered a poor country that had so much oil that it was oozing out of the ground in many places. Amazingly, the oil in this country was not used to generate income for this poor country. Once again, outsiders became rich through the oil of that nation and it became a wasted resource of that poor nation. Indeed, experienced rich people do not feel sorry for poor people because many poor people simply waste what God has given them. This poor country, obviously, does not have the wisdom of the serpent. The serpent does not waste anything. It digests the head, the eyes, the brains, the hoofs, the horns, the flesh, the intestines and the tongue of the antelope it swallows. Poor countries and poor people often waste many things.

Why Rich People Do Not Feel Sorry for Poor People

Generally speaking, rich people do not feel sorry for poor people. Anyone who thinks that rich people feel sorry for poor people is immature and inexperienced. Deficient leaders go around visiting their rich colleagues, looking pitiful and helpless. Don't deceive yourself! Experienced men know that there are reasons why poor people continue to be poor. In addition, human selfishness will always cause the rich man to be more concerned about his toothache than about the poor man's life-threatening problems.

There are many reasons why rich people do not feel sorry for poor people. If rich people felt sorry for poor people they would give more money and try to help in many more ways. Over time, rich people have discovered that poor people do have a lot of resources and opportunities but waste them and do not use them wisely! Many rich people have resigned from trying to help poor people. Why is that?

1. **Rich people do not feel sorry for poor people because poor people leave their lights on whilst rich people turn off their lights.** The lights on bridges and monuments in the great cities of the Western world are turned off in the night and not left to burn after midnight when no one will see them. One night, I was out in Darling Harbour in Sydney, Australia. At a certain time, the numerous lights on the bridges and monuments suddenly went off. I thought to myself, "These rich people are turning off their lights." I am sure that in certain poor countries thousands of lights were still burning strong even though they did not have a sure electricity supply.

2. **Rich pastors do not feel sorry for poor pastors because poor pastors are usually not concerned about improving their low income through their offerings.** Rich people are concerned about little sums of money because they add up to make huge sums of money. Jesus Christ gathered up the crumbs whilst irresponsible leaders allow everything to be wasted. Some Christians once mocked at me for receiving special coin offerings. I marveled because they were in debt and I was not!

3. **Rich people do not feel sorry for poor people because poor people chase after fantasies.** "...but he that followeth after vain persons shall have poverty enough" (Proverbs 28:19).

   Leaders of poor countries are specialists of travelling to rich countries to ask for help and loans. They chase fantasies whilst good leaders stay in their own countries, ensuring that practical things are done. Pastors with undeveloped church buildings love to travel around, spending a lot of time moving between America and Europe, but never developing their own local church.

4. **Rich people do not feel sorry for poor people because many poor people do not use their good seasons well.** In the season of fat cows they did not invest properly. It

is sad to see poor people who once had great opportunities and earned lots of money. Somehow, they did not use the good season properly and it passed before they could say, "Jack Robinson!" I know a country that had lots of cocoa, timber, gold and diamonds. These things had been harvested for years but had amounted to nothing for this country. This is why rich people do not feel sorry for poor people because they know that the poor people have misused their opportunities and wasted their resources. The good season when there were abundant forests and the mines were filled with gold and diamonds is past and that nation has no roads, no water and no electricity!

5. **Rich people do not feel sorry for poor people because many poor people are lazy.** Proverbs teaches that it is easy to *see the field of a lazy person* (a sluggard). I am not saying that all poor people are lazy. But I have noticed how some people stay in poverty because they do not want to work hard. Phlegmatic people are often too lazy to lift up themselves and do their work. I have also watched people work hard and rise out of difficulty. A lazy person always has a reason for not achieving his targets. The notion that poverty is caused by laziness is very biblical. King Solomon observed this phenomenon and recorded it.

I passed by THE FIELD OF THE SLUGGARD and by the vineyard of the man lacking sense, And behold, it was completely overgrown with thistles; its surface was covered with nettles, and its stone wall was broken down.

When I saw, I reflected upon it; I looked, and received instruction.

"A little sleep, a little slumber, a little folding of the hands to rest,"

Then your poverty will come as a robber and your want like an armed man.

Proverbs 24:30-34 (NASB)

6. **Rich people do not feel sorry for poor people because many poor people and poor nations do things that do not make sense.** When you watch the news you wonder whether the leaders are thinking about the nation they are leading. Things that are obvious are allowed to go on, encouraging insurrectionists to overthrow governments. It is easy to see when a nation is being led by people who lack common sense. That nation always tends to poverty. Rich people and rich nations do not feel sorry for these poor nations because many senseless things are done by politicians who do not really love the nations they are leading.

I passed by the field of the sluggard and by the vineyard of THE MAN LACKING SENSE,

And behold, it was completely overgrown with thistles; its surface was covered with nettles, and its stone wall was broken down.

When I saw, I reflected upon it; I looked, and received instruction.

"A little sleep, a little slumber, a little folding of the hands to rest,"

Then your poverty will come as a robber and your want like an armed man.

Proverbs 24:30-34 (NASB)

7. **Rich people do not feel sorry for poor people because poor people seem to want bad leaders to perpetuate their disorganisation and confusion**. Indeed, good leaders are rarely chosen by the poor masses. Real leaders are often rejected as being harsh and difficult. Politics, good looks and good speeches may win an election. But politics, good looks and good speeches do not bring organisation and development. Hard leadership is what brings development and prosperity. Strong hard leadership in Singapore made that nation one of the richest in the world.

When God was creating the heavens and the earth, He separated light and darkness in order to bring out His beautiful creation.

...and God divided the light from the darkness.

Genesis 1:4

...and let it divide the waters from the waters.

Genesis 1:6

If you live in a disorganised and poor country, you will be amazed by the response you get when you try to bring some order into the confusion. Men will rise up to fight you and others will hate you for your suggestions. You will be accused of unbearable things for trying to help.

Most rich outsiders will learn to leave the poor people to live in their filth and confusion. Many poor countries have kiosks everywhere, tables everywhere, sign boards everywhere, cars parked everywhere, cars being sold everywhere, markets on the streets, sellers occupying roads, spoilt cars parked on major roads, gutters and drains filled with plastic bags and filth, rubbish dumps at every corner, and no one apparently in charge of anything! This confusion and disorganisation is perpetuated when the poor people choose fatally deficient men to lead them. Indeed good leaders are rarely chosen by poor masses.

CHAPTER 12

Masters of Hiding
and Flourishing

… he that refraineth his lips is wise.

Proverbs 10:19

Serpents Are Wise Because
They Hide And Flourish

If there is a lion living in your area, you are likely to hear about it. Most animals make some kind of noise, alerting us to their existence. Even mosquitoes announce their presence. Snakes rarely make any noise. Snakes are wise because they live in silence, rarely disturbing anyone. It is rare for us to see a snake and to hear any noise although it is there. Because of this great wisdom key, snakes flourish and prosper more than any other wild animal.

...therefore let thy words be few.

Ecclesiastes 5:2

Snakes are masters at hiding. Most of the time, the patterns of the snake's skin camouflage the snake by breaking up its outline and making it difficult for predators to see where the animal's body begins and ends.

A striped snake, for example, may look quite noticeable on the pavement but almost disappear when placed on the forest floor where it lives. These masters of hiding, blend with their environment until you do not notice them anymore. These characteristics give snakes the ability to hide and flourish. They prosper mainly because they are hidden from the view of others. *While snakes are hiding, they are flourishing, prospering and multiplying.*

A snake charmer in Bangladesh once found 3,500 poisonous cobras and their eggs hidden underneath the floors of two suburban homes. Imagine that, 3,500 cobras flourishing under the boards of your living room!

A huge viper was recently discovered on one of our building sites. When I saw pictures of this viper, I had goose bumps all over me. It was so large and so frightening and I knew that this snake should be nowhere else but in a zoo.

Where are dangerous animals kept? They are either out in the wild or confined to a zoo. But this dangerous viper had been living near human beings and flourishing. It had probably gotten married and had several children over the years. How was it able to hide and flourish? Through the master key of silence! Silence is a powerful weapon that allows you to truly hide, flourish and prosper.

Silence, Quietness, Hiding and Flourishing

1. **Hiding and flourishing is a godly practice.**

   God Himself hides from us! Why does God hide from us? Because of our pride and presumption. It humbles us and makes us seek Him until we find Him. Learning to hide is to become an imitator of God. Have you ever wondered why the Bible teaches, "Remove thy foot from thy neighbour's house lest he be weary of thee and so hate thee?" The more you are seen, the more you are despised. That is why removing your foot from your neighbour's house is important. You are more respected and valued because you hide yourself!

   Truly, You are a God who hides Himself, O God of Israel, Savior!

   Isaiah 45:15 (NASB)

2. **Quietness and silence will cause you to command the respect of outsiders.**

   Most people are uneasy around quiet people. When there is a meeting, a quiet person is often asked his opinion. He is often respected more because of his posture. If you want people to respect you, learn to keep quiet. The serpent that lies quietly in the grass without making a sound is one of the most feared and respected animals in the world.

...make it your ambition to lead a quiet life: You should mind your own business and work with your hands, just as we told you, so that your daily life MAY WIN THE RESPECT OF OUTSIDERS and so that you will not be dependent on anybody.

1 Thessalonians 4:11-12 (NIV)

3. **Hiding and flourishing will protect you from premature exposure in the ministry.**

Today, most pastors love to advertise and show their faces to the world. Advertisement is good and it has its positive effects. But when you are loud when you should be silent, you are endangering your very life and ministry. A certain level of exposure is not necessary all the time. When Jesus' ministry was exposed it was just a matter of time until He was killed. This is the reason why He limited His exposure until a certain point. Do not think that you need to be seen and known by everyone all the time. There is a time to be quiet and silent and there is a time to be seen.

"The world cannot hate you, but it hates Me because I testify of it, that its deeds are evil.

"Go up to the feast yourselves; I do not go up to this feast because My time has not yet fully come." Having said these things to them, He stayed in Galilee.

John 7:7-9 (NASB)

4. **Quietness will qualify you to work for very important people.**

Most important people would not like to have a blabber mouth near them. People who talk too much cannot work in sensitive places. Daniel, Shadrach, Meshach and Abednego were judged to be people who could stand in the king's palace. Do you want to work at the highest level? Then learn to shut up and not chat about everything you see or hear!

Pastors must not work with people who talk too much. It is not everything that has to be discussed, described or re-described.

Children in whom was no blemish, but well favoured, and skillful in all wisdom, and cunning in knowledge, and understanding science, and SUCH AS HAD ABILITY IN THEM TO STAND IN THE KING'S PALACE, and whom they might teach the learning and the tongue of the Chaldeans.

Daniel 1:4

5. Silence will help you to hear from God.

"Be still and know that I am God:..." (Psalm 46:10). This popular scripture is telling you to be silent and quiet so that you can hear from God.

Many times, Christians do not hear from God because they are too busy talking, chatting or singing. I once spoke to a millionaire who got saved in prison. I asked him why he waited until he went to prison before he got saved. He explained, "When you are out of prison, there are so many people to interact with. When I was in prison I had no one to talk to and no meetings to attend. It was there I began to commune with God."

You will definitely hear from God when you cut out the chatting, the talking and the human interaction. Notice the scripture below. It was when there was silence that he heard the voice of God.

Then a spirit passed before my face; the hair of my flesh stood up: It stood still, but I could not discern the form thereof: an image was before mine eyes, THERE WAS SILENCE, AND I HEARD A VOICE, SAYING, shall mortal man be more just than God? Shall a man be more pure than his maker?

Job 4:15-17

6. **Quietness and silence reveal your wisdom.**

A silent person is always seen as wise and respectable. Talking, chatting and relating do not make you look as wise as when you are quiet. A person who keeps quiet seems to have assessed the situation and judged that it is better to be quiet now than to speak. This is what seems to make him look wise.

A time to get, and a time to lose; a time to keep, and a time to cast away; a time to rend, and a time to sew; A TIME TO KEEP SILENCE, and a time to speak;

Ecclesiastes 3:6-7

7. **Quietness and silence will help you develop into a prophet.**

Amazingly, you will need to learn how to be quiet if you want to be a prophet of God. Apostle Paul was caught up into paradise and saw and heard wonderful things. But he made a remarkable comment about the things he saw and heard. *He said it was unlawful for him to say what he heard and saw.*

Indeed, if you need quietness and silence to work for important men, you will need quietness and silence to work for God. God can reveal things to you that He has no intention of sharing with the public. God is looking for friends whom He can chat with. Would you like it if everything you said to your friend was broadcast on a radio? If you are going to become a prophet of God, you will have to learn to be quiet. I once shared a revelation that God gave to me and I got into such trouble from doing that. I learnt quietness and silence the hard way.

It is not expedient for me doubtless to glory. I will come to visions and revelations of the Lord. I knew a man in Christ above fourteen years ago, (whether in the

body, I cannot tell; or whether out of the body, I cannot tell: God knoweth;) such an one caught up to the third heaven. And I knew such a man, (whether in the body, or out of the body, I cannot tell: God knoweth;) How that he was caught up into paradise, and heard unspeakable words, WHICH IT IS NOT LAWFUL FOR A MAN TO UTTER.

2 Corinthians 12:1-4

8. Silence is the way to deal with your accusers.

Therefore the prudent shall keep silence in that time; for it is an evil time.

Amos 5:13

Jesus could speak for hours when He was in the presence of friends but when He was in the presence of His enemies he was silent. You must learn to hold your peace when you stand in the presence of your accusers. Let them say what they can, but entrust yourself to God.

And the chief priests accused him of many things: but he answered nothing.

And Pilate asked him again, saying, ANSWEREST THOU NOTHING? Behold how many things they witness against thee. But Jesus yet answered nothing; so that Pilate marvelled.

Mark 15:3-5

9. Silence will help you not to sin with your mouth.

Developing the art of being quiet and silent will help you to avoid falling into many sins. It is easy to criticize! It is easy to be treacherous! It is easy to murmur! It is easy to grumble! Sin is present when there is a lot of talking. Developing the art of keeping quiet will increase your level of holiness and sinlessness.

When there are many words, transgression is unavoidable, but he who restrains his lips is wise.

Proverbs 10:19 (NASB)

10. Hide and flourish by doing your unseen assignments.

Serpents grow longer, bigger and more powerful as they hide in the undergrowth. By the time you see a snake it may have lived near you for several years. How did it get to that size?

In the ministry the unseen work is prayer. There is plenty of unseen work for a priest. Notice the many unseen jobs that Eleazar the priest had to do.

And to the office of Eleazar the son of Aaron the priest pertaineth the oil for the light, and the sweet incense, and the daily meat offering, and the anointing oil, and the oversight of all the tabernacle, and of all that therein is, in the sanctuary, and in the vessels thereof.

Numbers 4:16

A modern pastor must be a master of the unseen and hidden jobs of ministry. The work of prayer! The work of intercession! The work of waiting on the Lord! The work of meeting leaders! The work with small groups! Most of these activities are hidden. But they are the most potent and fruitful activities of a minister. One day someone asked me, "Where did you get all these pastors from? When did they join your church?" He did not know about the many private meetings I have held, talking with young people and encouraging them to work for the Lord. It is this unseen aspect of the ministry that yields great fruit.

But thou, when thou prayest, enter into thy closet, and when thou hast shut thy door, pray to thy Father which is in secret; and thy Father which seeth in secret shall reward thee openly.

Matthew 6:6

CHAPTER 13

Masters of Self-Defence

**Take heed unto thyself, …thou shalt both save thyself,
…**

1 Timothy 4:16

Serpents Are Wise Because They Are Masters Of Self-Defence

Most snakes will not attack you if you leave them alone. However, they will rise up fiercely to kill anyone who threatens their existence. They are indeed masters of self-defence. It is this famous defensive response to danger that has given serpents their fearful reputation. Paul taught Timothy to guard himself and to defend himself. That is the wisdom of a serpent. Take heed to yourself and save yourself!

It was this self-defending attitude of David that Hushai the Archite spoke about when he advised Absalom not to pursue his father in the night. He warned him about his father's reaction to being surrounded and threatened. Absalom knew what Hushai the Archite was talking about. He knew that David was an expert at fighting back and extinguishing enemies in such a way that they would never be heard of again.

> **For, said Hushai, thou knowest thy father and his men, that they be mighty men, and they be chafed in their minds, AS A BEAR ROBBED OF HER WHELPS in the field: and thy father is a man of war, and will not lodge with the people.**
>
> **Behold, he is hid now in some pit, or in some other place: and it will come to pass, when some of them be overthrown at the first, that whosoever heareth it will say, There is a slaughter among the people that follow Absalom.**
>
> **And he also that is valiant, whose heart is as the heart of a lion, shall utterly melt: for all Israel knoweth that thy father is a mighty man, and they which be with him are valiant men.**
>
> **2 Samuel 17:8-10**

Every minister must develop a proper attitude towards enemies. This attitude is necessary to defend himself and the church properly. A certain ferocity is needed to fight enemies of the church who destroy the man of God. Anyone who does not have a certain ferocious attitude towards disloyalty will allow terrible works of the enemy to flourish among them until the church is destroyed. David reacted to enemies with a certain ferocity. When he was surrounded he determined to cut off his enemies in such a way that they would never be seen again.

You must learn to extinguish your enemies in a fire of thorns. Rise up fiercely and develop a spiritual reputation for self-defence. King David promised to extinguish his enemies, as a man would burn a heap of thorns! He would deal with them ferociously and fiercely and they would regret ever threatening him! He said, "They surrounded me like bees; they were extinguished as a fire of thorns; in the name of the Lord I will surely cut them off" (Psalm 118:12 NASB).

1. Defend Yourself Against Disloyalty

1. *Defend yourself against disloyal people by being conscious of the traits and patterns of disloyal men.* You must react to disloyalty! Don't be phlegmatic! Rise up and defend yourself against the threat of disloyalty!

. You must then mark and avoid such people so that their venom will be rendered powerless. "Now I beseech you, brethren, mark them which cause divisions and offences contrary to the doctrine which ye have learned; and avoid them. For they that are such serve not our Lord Jesus Christ, but their own belly; and by good words and fair speeches deceive the hearts of the simple" (Romans 16:17-18).

2. *Defend yourself against disloyal people by casting out scorners who do not really believe in you.* Dismissals, transfers, rotation of people are all important strategies of self-defence. You must be a master of self-defence if you are to build the church successfully. "Cast out the scorner,

and contention shall go out; yea, strife and reproach shall cease" (Proverbs 22:10).

3. *Defend yourself against disloyal associates by continuously teaching against the bad and poisonous behaviour of disloyalty.* Teaching has a real effect and it is powerful in fighting imaginations and thoughts that exalt themselves against the will of God. "Casting down imaginations, and every high thing that exalteth itself against the knowledge of God, and bringing into captivity every thought to the obedience of Christ" (2 Corinthians 10:5).

4. *Defend yourself against disloyal associates by keeping a private life and not revealing everything about yourself.* Treacherous people want something to talk about. The more they know about you, the more opportunity they have to attack you.

2. Defend Yourself Against Poverty

1. *Defend yourself against poverty by being a diligent hard worker who works more than eight hours a day.* Poverty comes like a traveler who has nowhere else to stay. Financial problems come like armed robbers who are bent on harming you. "So shall thy poverty come as one that travelleth, and thy want as an armed man" (Proverbs 6:11). You must rise up to defend yourself against poverty that is determined to overwhelm you. Defend yourself against poverty by working hard.

2. *Defend yourself against poverty by paying your tithes and avoiding the curses of those who do not pay their tithes.* "Honour the Lord with thy substance, and with the firstfruits of all thine increase: So shall thy barns be filled with plenty, and thy presses shall burst out with new wine" (Proverbs 3:9-10).

3. *Defend yourself against poverty by building your own house.* One day, you may not earn enough money to build a house. By then, you should have a roof over your head. "Through wisdom is an house builded; and by understanding it is established" (Proverbs 24:3). Be wise in your day of plenty and build a house as early as you can.

3. Defend Yourself Against Slow Destruction

Defend yourself against the slow deterioration around us. "For riches are not for ever: and doth the crown endure to every generation?" (Proverbs 27:24). There is a natural decline that is built into everything we do. From the moment you complete your house and move into it, it begins to decay. From the first day you use your new kitchen, it begins to deteriorate. Your marriage begins to decay from the moment you say "I do". Your church begins to decrease from the day you have your highest attendance. You must rise up and defend yourself against all forms of attrition. Defend yourself against the decay of the church by starting more branches and doing more outreaches. Defend your marriage by doing all the exciting things in the marriage books. Defend your house from decay by constantly repairing, renovating and improving things.

4. Defend Yourself Against Falsehood

Defend yourself against liars and deception. The world is full of deception and lies. The children of satan are dabbling in lies and deception all the time. A wise leader must expect people to lie to him. Through people's lies and falsehood you can be led astray. Defend yourself by demanding openness from all those that are close to you. Do not accept mysterious shadowy characters who do not say much when they are in your presence. "But if we walk in the light, as he is in the light, we have fellowship one with another, and the blood of Jesus Christ his Son cleanseth us from all sin" (1 John 1:7). God will give you grace and through the anointing no one will be able to deceive you. Those who think they are deceiving you will be the ones who will be deceived most. It is fun to deceive those who think they are deceiving you! "What shall be given unto thee? or what shall be done unto thee, thou false tongue? Sharp arrows of the mighty, with coals of juniper" (Psalm 120:3-4).

5. Defend Yourself Against Lust

1. *You must rise up and defend yourself against all forms of lust.* Every man is susceptible to lustful tendencies and sins. It is important to defend your mind, your body and your flesh against attacks of lust.

2. *Defend yourself against lust by winning the psychological battle of the mind.* Keep your thoughts pure and your conscience tender. "Lust not after her beauty in thine heart; neither let her take thee with her eyelids" (Proverbs 6:25).

3. *Defend yourself from the presence of strange women by the presence of your own wife, your sisters, your daughters or other good women.* A woman keeps away other women. A woman is the best protection from other women! "...Thou art my sister; and call understanding thy kinswoman: That they may keep thee from the strange woman..." (Proverbs 7:4-5).

4. *Defend yourself by not working with women at all if the only relationship you are used to having with women is a sexual one.* "For by means of a whorish woman a man is brought to a piece of bread: and the adulteress will hunt for the precious life" (Proverbs 6:26).

5. *Defend yourself against dangerous sexual fires and burns by getting married to a willing sexual partner.* You are done for, if your marriage partner is an unwilling sexual partner who just wants your sperms to create a legitimate baby for herself. Defend yourself against rising desires in marriage by constantly having sex with your wife. "… come together again, that Satan tempt you not for your incontinency" (1 Corinthians 7:5).

CHAPTER 14

Masters at Overcoming Demons

Behold, I GIVE UNTO YOU POWER TO TREAD ON SERPENTS and scorpions, AND OVER ALL THE POWER OF THE ENEMY: and nothing shall by any means hurt you. Notwithstanding in this rejoice not, that THE SPIRITS ARE SUBJECT UNTO YOU; but rather rejoice, because your names are written in heaven.

Luke 10:19-20

Serpents Are Wise Because They Eat Snakes

S ome snakes eat other snakes. Snakes are routinely killed by other snakes. Some poisonous snakes are merely a meal for other larger and less frightening serpents.

King cobras eat other snakes. Whereas boa constrictors, pythons, and other very large snakes sometimes eat calves, deer, and other big mammals, the king cobras eat almost all other snakes with the rat snake being its favourite meal. Indeed, the king cobra is peculiar in that it feeds almost exclusively on other snakes. The genus name of the king cobra is, "Ophiophagus" which means snake-eater.

Although the king cobra is known to attack larger snakes, including pythons, when food is scarce the king cobra will also feed on other small vertebrates, such as lizards. After a large meal the snake may live for many months without another meal due to its very slow metabolic rate.

Every pastor must be a master of demons. You must destroy satan.

You cannot allow evil spirits to be around you. You should be able to detect, feel and know when an evil spirit is present.

Be as wise as a serpent and overpower other evil spirits.

Special Demons that Every Minister Must Overcome

1. A minister must overcome evil spirits in his territory.

Every geographical area has invisible princes and thrones located there. These powerful spirits dominate the physical and spiritual environment of every location. When you arrive on the scene you must not be overcome by them but you must overcome them. There are places that are dominated by the spirit of divorce. If you do not defend yourself and attack these spirits, you will find yourself divorcing just because you have moved into that territory. There are areas that are dominated by the spirit of fornication. By simply relocating to live in such an area, you are exposed to terrible forces of lust and immorality.

It is important that you are aware of these realities and overcome the spirits which inhabit your area.

For we wrestle not against flesh and blood, but against PRINCIPALITIES, against POWERS, against the rulers of the darkness of this world, against spiritual wickedness in high places.

Wherefore take unto you the whole armour of God, that ye may be able to withstand in the evil day, and having done all, to stand.

Ephesians 6:12-13

2. A minister must overcome evil spirits in his appointees.

The commonest problem in appointees, employees and associates is pride. As you get used to your job and as you stay around longer, pride develops without your realising what is happening to you. Pride is the invisible enemy that slips in without anyone noticing. Lucifer was appointed as the chief worship director. It got into his head and he began to plan an overthrow of God Himself. It may sound fantastic but this is what happens all the time.

Someone you appoint begins to take everything for granted and assumes that he would have been there anyway. He does not realise that he has been given an opportunity that he must treasure. He must love and respect you for the rest of his life because of the opportunity you gave him. Surprisingly, many appointees turn around, betray and attack the very one who lifted them up. This is Lucifer's exact behaviour.

How art thou fallen from heaven, O Lucifer, son of the morning! How art thou cut down to the ground, which didst weaken the nations!

FOR THOU HAST SAID IN THINE HEART, I WILL ASCEND INTO HEAVEN, I will exalt my throne above the stars of God: I will sit also upon the mount of the congregation, in the sides of the north: I will ascend above the heights of the clouds; I will be like the most High.

YET THOU SHALT BE BROUGHT DOWN TO HELL, to the sides of the pit.

Isaiah 14:12-15

3. A minister must overcome evil spirits that oppose him. You will be opposed by evil spirits.

Satan is called the adversary, which means the one who opposes. A lot of resistance (both natural and spiritual) that you feel is actually caused by the presence of evil spirits who are sent to hinder and frustrate you. Computers that do not work, committees that turn against you, lights that go off and thieves that break in are all part of the opposition working against you.

Be sober, be vigilant; because your ADVERSARY the devil, as a roaring lion, walketh about, seeking whom he may devour.

1 Peter 5:8

4. A minister must overcome the evil spirits of familiarity.

Demons of familiarity are some of the most difficult to deal with because they operate through close associates, friends and relatives. Jesus Christ encountered strong resistance to His anointing through spirits of familiarity. Somehow, the people in his hometown did not believe in Him because they knew his family. Amazingly, his own family did not believe in Him. Now the Jews' feast of tabernacles was at hand.

His brethren therefore said unto him, Depart hence, and go into Judaea, that thy disciples also may see the works that thou doest. For there is no man that doeth any thing in secret, and he himself seeketh to be known openly. If thou do these things, shew thyself to the world. For NEITHER DID HIS BRETHREN BELIEVE IN HIM (John 7:2-5).

If you are as wise as a serpent you will overcome all these demons. Like the king cobra, the demons will simply be a meal. See my book "***Those Who Pretend***" for more insight on how to deal with the spirit of familiarity.

CHAPTER 15

Masters of Reputation

A good name is rather to be chosen than great riches…

Proverbs 22:1

Serpents Are Wise Because
They Generate Fear

The majority of snakes are either non-venomous or possess venom that is not harmful to humans. A snake only bites a person when threatened or alarmed. There are more serious injuries associated with using a chair than there are from snakes.

Horses kill more people than snakes do and yet horse riding remains a favourite pastime.

Can you believe that statistically more people are killed by bee-stings than by snakes?

In the United States alone over a thousand people are struck by lightning every year with around one hundred fatalities whilst there are only four to ten deaths from snakebites.

Serpents are masters at generating a fearful reputation. Snakes basically have a reputation of being killing machines.

The general public simply views a snake as a dangerous creature that must be killed. Being fearful of something that has the potential to harm you is quite normal. Being afraid of snakes is perfectly natural and shows the fearful reputation snakes have acquired.

Actually, only seven per cent of reported snake bites are due to accidentally being bitten. The major causes of snakebites are the following: trying to kill the snake; trying to catch the snake, trying to move the snake; trying to handle the snake and harassing the animal. So you can see that very few people are actually accidentally bitten by snakes.

Serpents have built up a fearful reputation that is difficult to dislodge. Deep fear of snakes, stems from their reputation for aggression, speed and venom toxicity. The reputation of snakes also comes from stories and legends that have been passed down from generation to generation.

There are many stories and legends about the black mamba, which give it an awesome and fearsome reputation. Some people claim that the black mamba can bite its tail to make a hoop, so that it will be able to roll down a mountain. As the mamba gets to the bottom of the mountain, it straightens its body out like a missile and attacks at high speed! You wouldn't want to meet one of those.

Another story about the black mamba claims that it has such high intelligence, enabling it to plot an attack on humans. It is said to ambush a car by waiting along the road. The black mamba will then coil itself around the wheel of the automobile to strike at the driver when he gets home.

Another popular story claims that the black mamba can balance its entire body at the tip of its tail.

When the black mamba is cornered, it will stand its ground and display incredible aggressive behaviour. A group of people is usually required to kill it, as it is quite fast and agile, striking in all directions almost at the same time People are known to have died within twenty minutes of being bitten by a black mamba. I assure you, you would not want to meet one of these black mambas!

 But did you know that bees kill more people than snakes every year? Did you know that horses kill more people than snakes but somehow do not inspire such fear and terror in human beings? Such is the power of a reputation, whether good or bad!

It is important to build up a good reputation by building up a history of accomplishments. You must generate faith in your followers by doing the things you say you will do. No matter how the statistics put it, snakes have a strong history of killing accomplishments. That is why they are feared! A recent study reveals that 5million people in the world are bitten each year by snakes. Of those 40,000 die. In India alone, 15,000 die every year from snake bites. These facts would inspire fear in anyone.

Politicians all over the world have built up a reputation of promising things they cannot and will not do. Many politicians have built up a reputation of pretence, corruption and wickedness. The voter turn-out statistics of every country reveals how little faith people have in politicians. Their reputation is at the lowest ever.

King David's reputation was built on solid achievements that he had chalked. He was the one who had killed Goliath the giant. No one could take that away from him. "And it came to pass as they came, when David was returned from the slaughter of the Philistine, that the women came out of all cities of Israel, singing and dancing, to meet king Saul, with tabrets, with joy, and with instruments of musick. And the women answered one another as they played, and said, Saul hath slain his thousands, and David his ten thousands" (1 Samuel 18:6-7).

Be a man of your word and you will build a good reputation for doing what you said you would do. When you raise money, make sure you use it for what you said you would. If you said you would have a crusade, make sure that you have it. If you said you would build a church make sure that you build it. Do what you said you would do and build for yourself a strong reputation.

CHAPTER 16

Masters of Living Peaceably with Men

. . . live peaceably with all men.

Romans 12:18

Serpents Are Wise Because They Can Live Peacefully With Men

S nakes are masters at avoiding conflict and confrontation - until necessary. When they cannot avoid confrontation, they attack. This is why you have probably found a snake in your house before. That snake has been in your house for years. It lived peacefully with human beings, even though human beings hate snakes with a passion.

All through the bible the scripture encourages us to live peacefully and quietly with all men. You cannot do much for God if you do not know how to make peace and live in peace. It's time to learn from the serpent how to live peacefully with the very people who want to kill you. "And the fruit of righteousness is sown in peace of them that make peace" (James 3:18).

For the most part, snakes either freeze or flee when humans approach. If a person comes too close, however, many will bite. Fortunately, most species are not venomous, and the bite only serves to surprise the person rather than hurt him or her.

It is important that you develop the art of living peacefully with all the different groups of people in your world.

1. **If you are wise as a serpent you will live peaceably with your brothers and sisters.**

   Leave there thy gift before the altar, and go thy way; first be reconciled to thy brother, and then come and offer thy gift.

   Matthew 5:24

Jesus insists that you must be reconciled to your brothers before you worship Him. That is a basic Christian requirement. Some families are always having one conflict or another. There is always one problem or another between Christian brothers and sisters. If you are a Christian, it is important that you distance yourself from conflicts that get nowhere. Rise up and display your maturity by refusing to live in conflict with anybody. A condition for God to accept your sacrifice is for you to make peace with your brethren.

2. If you are wise as a serpent you will live peaceably with your spouse.

Live joyfully with the wife whom thou lovest all the days of the life of thy vanity, which he hath given thee under the sun, all the days of thy vanity: for that is thy portion in this life, and in thy labour which thou takest under the sun.

Ecclesiastes 9:9

How can you live joyfully with your wife if you are always quarrelling with her? Perhaps you are not as wise as a serpent that is why you live in conflict for longs periods of time. Do not let the sun go down on your anger! End your quarrel by 5.30pm.

It is important to measure the level of peace you enjoy with your spouse. Some marriages are constantly in conflict. Unfortunately, some couples are terribly mismatched and so constantly live in discord. Some men cannot help but point out more and more faults in their wives. They are unable to overlook the smallest mistakes and constantly see themselves as school teachers sent to correct and train their woman. This kind of thinking leads to perpetual conflict as the spouse does not see herself as a student in a school.

Some men are in conflict with their wives because they compare her with better looking options around. They therefore manifest their discontentment by finding fault with their wives. Whatever the reason, you must see constant conflict as a dangerous sign in your life. Even when there are serious disagreements, it is possible to live peacefully with your spouse.

Another unfortunate cause of marital conflict is when the couple try to do everything together. God did not make couples into Siamese twins. Siamese twins are linked together at every moment and every second of their lives. Siamese twins are some of the most miserable beings on earth because they never have a moment of independence or privacy. Siamese twins are known to prefer death to their continued existence together.

When I got married, I wanted to do everything with my wife and I found that it created a lot of conflict. I became happier when I allowed her to be herself and I allowed myself to be myself. Try doing things as individuals, just as you did before you got married and you may have more joy and peace.

3. **If you are wise as a serpent you will live peacefully with other ministers.**

Who are you in conflict with? How many people are there whom you do not talk to? How can you be a Christian and always have someone you do not flow with or talk to? That is not good Christian behaviour. Many ministers of the gospel are known for their conflicts that they have with each other. Sometimes, the conflicts spill over into the public domain and their church members get involved. Abraham did not want to have such a conflict with Lot. He did not want his herdsmen or his followers to fight the other camp. He did not want his herdsmen to be in conflict with someone else's herdsmen. Many pastors are happy when their church members are in conflict with other people's church members. They fuel the rivalry from behind. That is not how to live peacefully with fellow ministers of the gospel. Even government officials know about conflicts between churches and remark that the church of God is divided.

> And Abram said unto Lot, Let there be no strife, I pray thee, between me and thee, and between my herdmen and thy herdmen; for we be brethren.
>
> Genesis 13:8

4. **If you are wise as a serpent you will live peacefully with all men.**

> Recompense to no man evil for evil. Provide things honest in the sight of all men. If it be possible, as much as lieth in you, LIVE PEACEABLY WITH ALL MEN.
>
> Romans 12:17-18

Make it your aim to live peacefully with all the people God brings into your life. Live peacefully with the government! Live peacefully with the opposition party! Live peacefully with your neighbours! Live peaceably with the church!

CHAPTER 17

Masters at Subduing Spouses

Wives, submit yourselves ...

Ephesians 5:22

Serpents Are Wise Because
They Can Subdue Their Spouses

There are snakes that eat up their mates. They suck them in like noodles. Imagine eating up your wife when you feel like it! When some snakes are about to mate, the female snake is wary because it is not sure if it will be eaten up afterwards!

A good husband must show his strength as a head. It is wisdom to be a strong and wise leader in the marriage. Surprisingly, one of the greatest causes of unhappiness in marriage is a weak husband. You would have thought that a strong husband would be overbearing and make his wife unhappy. Actually, it is the opposite.

Even the strongest women are looking for a stronger man who can dominate them, lead them, guide them, teach them and provide for them. Many strong-willed women are highly irritated by weak wishy-washy husbands who cannot make up their minds about anything. They are seeking a stronger personality that they can confidently call a head.

1. **If you are wise as a serpent you will command your household, including your spouse, to obey you.**

   It is God's wisdom to be a strong leader and a strong head of your household. Human beings are difficult to lead. Even God finds it difficult to win our hearts and to make us obey Him. It is no wonder that a man should struggle to lead his wife.

   Since the days of Abraham, the ability to lead your own home has been used as a litmus test for good leadership. "For I know him, that he will command his children and his household after him, and they shall keep the way of the LORD, to do justice and judgment; that the Lord may bring upon Abraham that which he hath spoken of him" (Genesis 18:19). Today, in the ministry, the apostle Paul uses the same yardstick to determine whether a person is fit to lead a church.

One that ruleth well his own house, having his children in subjection with all gravity;

1 Timothy 3:4

2. If you are wise as a serpent, you will not allow your wife to make you have sex with another woman (directly or indirectly, overtly or subtly).

Amazingly, many Christian wives actually lead their husbands to have affairs with other women. This is what Sarai did when she encouraged Abraham to go into her maid.

Now Sarai Abram's wife bare him no children: and she had an handmaid, an Egyptian, whose name was Hagar. And Sarai said unto Abram, Behold now, the LORD hath restrained me from bearing: I pray thee, go in unto my maid; it may be that I may obtain children by her. And Abram hearkened to the voice of Sarai.

Genesis 16:1-2

You must realise that there are two kinds of marriages: marriages between committed Christians and marriages between Christians and unbelievers. In Christian marriages, the balance of power shifts to the woman and she may behave badly, knowing that her committed Christian husband will not and cannot go outside the marriage.

When it is a marriage between a Christian and an unbeliever, the balance of power shifts to the man. He is uncontrolled because he knows he can go from girl to girl seeking pleasure. Usually, Christian women married to unbelievers are humble, soft, dedicated and malleable, knowing that their husbands are uncontrollable.

Very poor and unwilling sexual performances from so-called committed Christian wives are a subtle way of driving their husbands into the arms of other women. These Christian wives are silently urging their spouses to find someone else.

Sometimes, wives of committed Christian men travel away to live in other countries for months on end. Some husbands even allow their wives to live elsewhere for years. If you are wise as a serpent, you will subdue your spouse. You will not allow her to do things that will destroy both of you.

3. **If you are wise as a serpent you will not allow your wife to make you eliminate people God has put in your life.**

You must subdue the woman who makes you eliminate the important people in your life. Jezebel is famous for how she eliminated Naboth! But Jezebel is not the only woman to eliminate people she does not want! Many ladies, out of their insecurity, eliminate people they do not like! It is not uncommon to find a long list of ladies who have been eliminated due to the pressure wives placed on their husbands.

The Jezebel spirit is callous and unfeeling, not caring what happens to those who are eliminated. Jezebel did not care what happened to Naboth! He could go to hell, as far as she was concerned. She organised the elimination of somebody's father, brother and son. The voice of Jezebel rings loud and strong today, "Let her go. Let him go, I don't want to see them anymore. I don't care what happens to them. I don't care if they do not have a ministry anymore. I don't care if they do not have a job anymore. Just let them go out of my sight."

And it came to pass, when Jezebel heard that Naboth was stoned, and was dead, that Jezebel said to Ahab, Arise, take possession of the vineyard of Naboth the Jezreelite, which he refused to give thee for money: for Naboth is not alive, but dead.

1 Kings 21:15

4. **If you are wise as a serpent you will not allow your wife to lead you away from your ministry.**

    This is what happened to Solomon. You must subdue or reject the woman who leads you away from God. Unfortunately, some men allow their wives to lead them away from their ministry. I remember a couple I counselled about a decision they were taking to leave the church. Initially, it looked as though the husband could be persuaded to do the right thing. However, he completely turned away from the path of righteousness and went astray. It was mysterious to me because I perceived that he was listening to my counsel. Years later, I found out that his wife, although quiet during the meetings, was the strong influence behind the scenes, urging him to resign and leave the church. Just like Solomon's wives, this lady had turned her husband's heart away from the ministry. Wives are powerful people. They can actually turn the direction of somebody's heart.

    But king Solomon loved many strange women ...

    For it came to pass, when Solomon was old, that HIS WIVES TURNED AWAY HIS HEART after other gods: and his heart was not perfect with the LORD his God, as was the heart of David his father.

    1 Kings 11:1, 4

5. **If you are wise as a serpent you will not allow your wife to make you disobey God.**

    You will make her obey God. You will notice that when the serpent came into the garden to tempt them, he did not talk to the man at all. He only spoke to the woman. The devil knew that he could get to the man through the woman. Because the Bible teaches husbands to love their wives, it is difficult for Christian husbands to be hard on their wives. Many Christian husbands end up disobeying God because they do not want to be hard on the wives they are supposed to subdue. Eve put pressure on her husband and made him disobey God. All the disasters of this world came into being because of this singular marital mistake. Are you making the same mistake today? Are you being soft when you are supposed to be hard? Look at the problems we have in our world today. It all came from a husband who was soft when he should have been hard.

... she took of the fruit thereof, and did eat, and gave also unto her husband with her; and he did eat. And the eyes of them both were opened, and they knew that they were naked; and they sewed fig leaves together, and made themselves aprons.

Genesis 3:6-7

6. If you are wise as a serpent you will rebuke your wife and put her in place when you have to.

You must subdue your wife with the strength that it requires. You must subdue the manipulative tendencies that rise within your spouse. David the king rebuked Michal and put her in place when she came huffing and puffing at the king for letting his clothes slip off whilst he was dancing. Many wives' unruly speeches and behaviour go unchecked.

Even pastors, seeking to remain in the good books of church members, do not rebuke these rebellious wives when they have to.

This results in the multiplication of rebelliousness in the women within the church. David had no difficulty in putting Michal in her place.

Another reason why unruly woman are left unchecked is because people cannot imagine that ugly behaviour can come from such beautiful women. Many beautiful women are actually ugly on the inside. All their softness and beauty is just a façade! Watch how David did it! That's the way to do it. Learn from king David. He was a man after God's own heart! Perhaps it was the way he handled his wife

Michal that made him a man after God's own heart. It was Abraham's ability to control his household that made God choose him. It is your ability to lead your household that qualifies you to be a bishop.

Then David returned to bless his household. And Michal the daughter of Saul came out to meet David, and said, How glorious was the king of Israel to day, who uncovered himself to day in the eyes of the handmaids of his servants, as one of the vain fellows shamelessly uncovereth himself!

And David said unto Michal, It was before the LORD, which chose me before thy father, and before all his house, to appoint me ruler over the people of the LORD, over Israel: therefore will I play before the LORD.

And I will yet be more vile than thus, and will be base in mine own sight: and of the maidservants which thou hast spoken of, of them shall I be had in honour.

2 Samuel 6:20-22

7. If you are wise as a serpent you will not allow your wife's tears and moods to guide you.

Then said Elkanah her husband to her, Hannah, why weepest thou? and why eatest thou not? and why is thy heart grieved? AM NOT I BETTER TO THEE THAN TEN SONS?

1 Samuel 1:8

It is dangerous to be guided or led by anything other than the Holy Spirit. The tears of a woman are not a substitute for the Holy Spirit. Pastors are tenderhearted and do not like to see people suffering. But a minister of the gospel must pledge himself to be led by the Holy Spirit and not by any other influence. It is new and immature husbands who are greatly moved by tears and sad moods! As you mature, you will come to realise that moods and tears can be used as weapons to manipulate the man of God. You will become wary of these weapons when they are deployed against you.

Do not be led by somebody's quietness, mood swings or gallons of tears. Be led by the Holy Spirit! Adam has gotten us into enough trouble by listening to his wife when he shouldn't have. Abraham has gotten this world into enough "terror" by listening to his wife when he shouldn't have. It is time that you become as wise as a serpent and subdue your spouse!

CHAPTER 18

Masters of Speed

And **GO QUICKLY**, and tell his disciples that he is risen from the dead; and, behold, he goeth before you into Galilee; there shall ye see him: lo, I have told you.

Matthew 28:7

And Moses said unto Aaron, Take a censer, and put fire therein from off the altar, and put on incense, and **GO QUICKLY** unto the congregation, and make an atonement for them: for there is wrath gone out from the LORD; the plague is begun.

Numbers 16:46

Serpents Are Wise Because They Move With Speed

Most snakes are feared because of their venomous bites. But the black mamba, which has been called 'death incarnate' by some biologists, has an even more fearsome reputation. It has been called the most dangerous snake in the world because of its aggression and speed. Certainly the black mamba is the most feared snake in Africa. Why is that?

The black mamba is very fast and agile. A group of people are usually required to kill it. When cornered, it strikes in all directions while a third of its body is suspended above the ground. Over short distances it can move at up to 5.4metres per second which is almost 20 kilometres per hour and faster than most people can sprint. The black mamba can travel with a third of its body raised off the ground and can move quickly on trees, on the ground or in water.

The speed and aggression of the black mamba make it one of the most successful snakes of all time. You will achieve great success if you learn to do things aggressively and with speed. Speed is a very important quality and most races and competitions exist to determine how fast you can go.

The strike of a snake is so fast that you may just feel the prick but never see the snake itself. Some vipers can go from being coiled up to opening its mouth, unfolding its fangs, lunging, biting and injecting venom to folding its fangs back again, closing its mouth and returning to a coiled up position in a fraction of a second. Like I said, the human eye cannot follow the strike. It is so swift!

So, what is the speed of your strike? What is the speed of your response to God's call? What is the speed of your obedience to the will of God? How swift are you when you are responding to God?

Most competitions exist to uncover and discover people's capacity for speed: the speed of dogs, the speed of horses, the speed of cars, the speed of planes and the speed of human beings! A lot of money can be earned if you are fast.

In the ministry, a lot of things also respond to speed. The slower you are, the more unsuccessful you will be in the work of God. To be wise as a serpent you must increase your speed! You must increase your speed in the many different areas of your life and ministry. In the next section, I want to show you certain critical areas where speed is important. You must critically increase your speed in all these areas.

Ten Areas to Increase Your Speed

1. Increase your speed by responding to your call quickly.

If God has called you, you must answer the call quickly and you must obey what God has said. Everything changes when there are delays. Everything changes when you do not respond quickly. If you read the bible you will discover many people who obeyed God immediately.

I have been a pastor for twenty-five years and I have encouraged many people to work for the Lord. Actually, my ministry has hinged around encouraging people to serve the Lord. The reality I have observed over the years is that people who do not quickly respond to the call of God eventually do not respond at all. All kinds of delays, slowness and excuses are the reasons why people do not end up in the ministry. You need to be quick to accept that God has called you. You need to be quick to obey His will for you!

When the apostle Paul received the call of God, he immediately began to preach. All those who do not start immediately end up not starting! A thousand excuses are given for not doing what is right, but the end result is the same. No speed, no ministry!

So Ananias departed and entered the house, and after laying his hands on him said, "Brother Saul, the Lord Jesus, who appeared to you on the road by which you were coming, has sent me so that you may regain your sight and be filled with the Holy Spirit."

And immediately there fell from his eyes something like scales, and he regained his sight, and he got up and was baptized; and he took food and was strengthened. Now for several days he was with the disciples who were at Damascus, and IMMEDIATELY HE BEGAN TO PROCLAIM JESUS in the synagogues, saying, "He is the Son of God."

Acts 9:17-20 (NASB)

2. Increase your speed by responding quickly to visions.

A vision appeared to Paul in the night: a man of Macedonia was standing and appealing to him, and saying, "Come over to Macedonia and help us."

WHEN HE HAD SEEN THE VISION, IMMEDIATELY WE SOUGHT TO GO into Macedonia, concluding that God had called us to preach the gospel to them.

So putting out to sea from Troas, we ran a straight course to Samothrace, and on the day following to Neapolis;

Acts 16:9-11 (NASB)

When the apostle Paul had the vision to go to Macedonia he responded immediately. What has God told you? What has He asked you to do? How many years are you going to take to do what you have been told to do? I am glad I obeyed the call of God when I was twenty-five years old. There have been many reasons why I should have done something else. Within a year of my medical training, I moved quickly into full time ministry. I have been in full time ministry all my working life. I have no regrets for starting early. There are many people who wish they had done what I did twenty years ago. They contemplated, they dreamt, they imagined but they never took the step.

Speed is important if you are to fulfil the will of the Lord.

3. Increase your speed by quickly leaving the world behind you.

Notice how Andrew and Peter left their fishing nets and followed Jesus. They did it immediately.

"As He was going along by the Sea of Galilee, He saw Simon and Andrew, the brother of Simon, casting a net in the sea; for they were fishermen. And Jesus said to them, 'Follow Me, and I will make you become fishers of men.' IMMEDIATELY, they left their nets and followed Him" (Mark 1:16-18 NASB).

Don't hesitate to leave your worldly friends behind. Don't hesitate to leave your old school mates behind. Don't hesitate to leave your old career behind. It is nothing! It is nothing! It is dung! I walked away from the world as soon as I finished my internship. I have no regrets that I did it so quickly.

4. Increase your speed by starting your ministry quickly.

Speed is most important when it comes to the start of your ministry. Ministry is a long road with many painful hurdles. No matter how you delay the start of the journey, the hurdles will remain in place, waiting for you to arrive there. If you wait too long, you will get to those hurdles when you are a worn out old man.

The hurdles will not have pity for you. The hurdles will not be lowered because of your age. The hurdles will not be reduced because you had a late start. The earlier and quicker you begin your ministry, the earlier and quicker you will get past certain hurdles. I am grateful to God for the chance I had to start a church whilst I was a student. Although I was just following my zealous love for the

Lord, I did not know that I was making one of the wisest moves of my whole life by starting quickly.

When Peter's mother in law was healed, she rose up and immediately began ministering. All examples of successful ministry involve people who rise up and start their ministry immediately.

Then He got up and left the synagogue, and entered Simon's home. Now Simon's mother-in-law was suffering from a high fever, and they asked Him to help her.

And standing over her, He rebuked the fever, and it left her; and SHE IMMEDIATELY GOT UP AND WAITED ON THEM.

While the sun was setting, all those who had any who were sick with various diseases brought them to Him; and laying His hands on each one of them, He was healing them.

Luke 4:38-40 (NASB)

5. Increase your speed of recognizing anointed people.

When they had crossed over they came to land at Gennesaret, and moored to the shore. When they got out of the boat, IMMEDIATELY THE PEOPLE RECOGNIZED HIM, and ran about that whole country and began to carry here and there on their pallets those who were sick, to the place they heard He was.

Wherever He entered villages, or cities, or countryside, they were laying the sick in the market places, and imploring Him that they might just touch the fringe of His cloak; and as many as touched it were being cured.

Mark 6:53-56 (NASB)

In the passage above, we see how the multitudes recognized the anointing and the anointed one. Because they recognized the anointing, they received their healing. Those who did not recognize the anointing, did not come out of their houses to receive a blessing.

Over the years I have treasured certain people because I recognized them as anointed men. People have wondered why I make a fuss about certain anointed men. If you are spiritual, you will recognize and respect people just because of the anointing on their lives. Sometimes it is not easy to recognize a great anointing. You must become sensitive to the anointing and recognize it quickly. Why is that? When you do not recognize anointed people quickly, you may criticize them instead. Anointed people are sent into your life at a particular season. They are also sent for a particular reason.

Kenneth Hagin was sent into my life so that I could receive an anointing and a ministry. Through the anointing on his life, I received a ministry and became anointed to do what I am doing. I loved his tapes so much and I enjoyed listening to his messages. I would share them with others but no one seemed to find them as special as I did. One night, in 1988, whilst listening to Kenneth Hagin, the power of God fell on me and I became anointed to teach. That teaching anointing has given me the opportunity to build churches, have conferences, conduct crusades, raise up pastors and do many other things. I pray for you that you will recognize anointed people when they are sent to you. You will miss your blessing if you do not quickly recognize people that are sent into your life.

6. Increase your speed of tackling the harvest.

And He was saying, "The kingdom of God is like a man who casts seed upon the soil;

and he goes to bed at night and gets up by day, and the seed sprouts and grows -- how, he himself does not know.

"The soil produces crops by itself; first the blade, then the head, then the mature grain in the head.

"But when the crop permits, HE IMMEDIATELY PUTS IN THE SICKLE, because the harvest has come."

Mark 4:26-29 (NASB)

Why was the Holy Spirit given? So that we will go out and be witnesses to the ends of the earth! When the church stops winning souls it falls into darkness and the Holy Spirit departs.

The harvest is waiting for you and for me. As Christians have dedicated themselves to rejoicing in affluent cities, other religions have crept in unawares and taken over vast regions of forgotten souls. Many pastors do not do any evangelism or crusades. "When I am as rich as those famous American evangelists, I will also do such things" they say. Be careful my friend. The blood of many unsaved people will be required at your hand. Souls are parting as we live today! Souls will part as the days go by! How many really will die in Christ? How many really will live again?

7. **Increase your speed by quickly moving away from those who reject you.**

Then the whole multitude of the country of the Gadarenes round about besought him to depart from them; for they were taken with great fear: and he went up into the ship, and returned back again.

Luke 8:37

Many people will not believe in you. Not everyone will believe in your call. You must be quick to turn away from those who do not believe in you, otherwise your real ministry will be quenched. There are always some people who love you, who like you and who want to hear you. Be quick to turn in that direction and avoid those who despise you.

8. **Increase your speed by being quick to detect disloyalty.**

Immediately Jesus, aware in his spirit that they were reasoning that way within themselves, said to them, "Why are you reasoning about these things in your hearts? "Which is easier, to say to the paralytic, "Your sins are forgiven"; or to say, "Get up, and pick up your pallet and walk"?

Mark 2:3-9 (NASB)

Another area you must develop swiftness in is your ability to detect disloyal, disgruntled and discontented people. Jesus Christ sensed the rejection and despisement in the Pharisees. When you do not detect and diagnose disloyalty quickly, it grows and infects others. Your whole church and ministry can be destroyed because you do not detect disloyalty quickly. To be quick at detecting disloyalty, see my book *Loyalty and Disloyalty,* especially the chapter on "Signs of Disloyalty".

9. **Increase your speed by being quick to identify potential leaders.**

Another important area where you must be fast is in identifying potential leaders. The leaders of tomorrow are all around you. The wonderful people you will need are all around you. In order to do well in ministry, you must identify potential leaders and great people around you. If you do not recognize them, another ministry will. Other people will identify the people you rejected and use them for great things. When you meet them, you will be amazed at what they have been trained to do. For more on how to identify potential leaders see my book, *The Art of Leadership.*

Going on a little farther, He saw James the son of Zebedee, and John his brother, who were also in the boat mending the nets. IMMEDIATELY HE CALLED THEM; and they left their father Zebedee in the boat with the hired servants, and went away to follow Him.

Mark 1:19-20 (NASB)

10. **Increase your speed by being quick to root out foolishness.**

"Call now, is there anyone who will answer you? And to which of the holy ones will you turn? "For anger slays the foolish man, and jealousy kills the simple. "I HAVE SEEN THE FOOLISH TAKING ROOT, AND I CURSED HIS ABODE IMMEDIATELY. "His sons are far from safety, they are even oppressed in the gate, and there is no deliverer.

Job 5:1-4 (NASB)

It is important to root out foolishness quickly. Disorderly, rebellious and disobedient people are dangerous because they have a way of spreading their poison. Many under-developed countries are poor because of a culture of allowing foolishness to take root. All sorts of things are allowed in the name of not offending people.

Visit a poor country and you will find roads meant for cars that are used as markets. Kiosks and containers line the pavements, forcing the pedestrians to walk on the roads.

Slums of shacks, kiosks and containers are allowed to expand and take over the city because politicians, fearing they may lose popularity, refuse to root out disorderliness.

In such countries, you will find the city authorities come up years after they should have prevented the development of these slums, to demolish and destroy poor people's homes, treating the people like animals. This unfortunate style of leadership is due to a lack of speed in those who lead.

CHAPTER 19

Masters at Operating
by the Senses

... those who have their senses exercised to discern
both good and evil.

Hebrews 5:14

Serpents Are Wise Because
They Operate By Their Senses

S nakes are marvellous creatures that live and move on the ground without the privilege of standing up to see what is happening around them. Yet, without the privilege of seeing what we see and hearing what we hear, and communicating like we do, they are able to live, eat, drink and avoid danger. They flourish where no other animal flourishes and they succeed where no other animal succeeds.

Like any professional assassin, a viper comes equipped with an arsenal of high-tech weaponry and extremely sensitive detection equipment.

The eyes of snakes are particularly good at detecting movement. It has special sound detectors. Rather than hearing sounds as we do, snakes pick up vibrations from the skin around their jaws.

Pit Vipers are named after their specialized thermo receptors; heat-sensitive organs, located on either side of the head that look like small pits. These pits contain membranes sensitive to infrared radiation and allow the snakes to locate their prey based on temperature differences with their environment.

A snake's tongue is also used to sense its surroundings. Snakes smell by using their forked tongues to collect airborne particles. The fork in the tongue gives the snake a sort of "directional sense of smell".

Snakes have no ears or movable eyelids. They do not hear airborne sound waves, but can perceive low-frequency vibrations transmitted from the ground to the bones of their skulls.

When a viper rests its jaw on the ground, any vibrations on the ground are amplified enormously. A snake can detect even the impact of a mouse's feet on sand. When a mouse moves within 15cm of the snake's head, a snake is bound to know that prey is within striking range.

All these facts reveal a creature that is very sensitive, perceiving all sorts of sensations and taking decisions based on them. Few creatures are so sensitive and accurate with what they perceive. We can learn a lot from this wisdom and begin to use our senses like God expects us to. Perhaps, we would live longer and achieve more if we were more perspicacious and sensitive.

Begin To Operate By Your Senses

1. Begin to sense the anointing when it is present.

And Jesus, immediately knowing in himself that virtue had gone out of him, turned him about in the press, and said, who touched my clothes?

And his disciples said unto him, thou seest the multitude thronging thee, and sayest thou, who touched me? And he looked round about to see her that had done this thing.

Mark 5:30-32

Jesus was sensitive! He knew when the anointing had gone out of Him. The anointing is the power of the Holy Spirit working through you. I used to hear people say, "Can you 'feel the presence' of God?" I did not know what they meant. I never knew whether I was feeling the presence of God or not. "What exactly is the presence of God?" I thought.

One day, I was ministering in Europe and had no intention of having a miracle service. I suddenly felt the presence of God and knew that miracles were taking place. When I called out for testimonies, many amazing miracles had taken place.

From that day, I knew that "sensing" the anointing was real. Perhaps you have never sensed the presence of God. Tune yourself, and make yourself ready to sense the anointing. Nowadays, even when chatting with people, I may sense the presence of God. Sometimes, when talking to an individual I may sense the power of God. Don't be dull and dry! You can become sensitive to the anointing!

2. Begin to sense when people don't have faith in you.

And they reasoned among themselves, saying, it is because we have taken no bread.

Which when Jesus perceived, he said unto them, o ye of little faith, why reason ye among yourselves, because ye have brought no bread?

Matthew 16:7-8

You must be sensitive to the faith or doubts of your disciples. Not everyone believes in everything you are saying and doing. Sometimes, I sense a lack of confidence coming from certain individuals. As a good leader, you must recognize the different levels of confidence in the people around you. You must not be deluded about how much you are loved and how much you are trusted. You must think maturely, sensing doubt when there is doubt and sensing fear when there is fear!

3. Begin to sense when people have faith in you and in your ministry.

And, behold, men brought in a bed a man which was taken with a palsy: and they sought means to bring him in, and to lay him before him.

And when they could not find by what way they might bring him in because of the multitude, they went upon the housetop, and let him down through the tiling with his couch into the midst before Jesus.

And WHEN HE SAW THEIR FAITH, he said unto him, Man, thy sins are forgiven thee.

Luke 5:18-20

Why is it important to notice when people have faith in you? Because you must spend your time ministering to those who have faith in you. You must go where people believe in you! You must spend time with people who trust you.! You must avoid those who do not like you and believe in you! Do not deceive yourself that everyone likes you or believes in you! God has chosen certain people to like you, to trust you and to have faith in you. Begin to perceive and pick up these little differences that make a big difference.

Many pastors are sad when there are no miracles. Most of us are depressed when there seems to be no anointing and no flow of the Spirit. We often blame ourselves for the lack of joy and the lack of a powerful anointing. Perhaps, you did not pray enough? Perhaps you did not fast? Perhaps you committed a sin, so God has withheld His power! These are some of the thoughts that go through our minds when we do not sense the presence of God. However, with time you will learn that the flow of the anointing depends more on the people you are ministering to than on yourself. If the people are hungry for God and have faith in your ministry, the power of God will flow.

Remember that Jesus could not do miracles in His own hometown. The Son of God Himself could not do miracles because the people were sceptical. If the Son of God was limited by the congregation, how much more you and I?

One day, the Lord appeared in a vision to a great prophet and gave him a gift. The instructions He gave to the prophet were interesting. He said to him, "Tell the people I appeared to you! Tell the people I gave you a gift! If they believe that I appeared to you, the anointing will flow into them and they will be healed."

I always wondered, "Why did the prophet have to say, 'Jesus appeared to me'?"

The answer is simple. It is important for people to believe in God and also to believe in the vessel who is ministering. Indeed, the faith of the congregation is very important. It is even more important than the minister's faith! Begin to sense and assess the faith of the people you are speaking to.

The apostle Paul sensed when people around him had faith in his ministry. This is a very important thing to sense when you are in the ministry. Paul perceived that the man had faith for healing, and then he moved!

The same heard Paul speak: who stedfastly beholding him, and perceiving that he had faith to be healed, Said with a loud voice, Stand upright on thy feet...

Acts 14:9-10

4. Begin to sense when there are wicked people around.

Jesus Christ sensed the wickedness of the people around Him. Never think that everybody loves you. Many people have wicked intentions. There are many wicked people who pretend to be interested in you! They may seek to interview you and find out more about the Bible. These people who were interviewing Jesus were actually asking theological questions. But they hated Jesus Christ and were only interested in finding fault with Him.

Jesus was wise as a serpent. He sensed the wickedness of his interviewers. Are you as wise as a serpent? Are your senses exercised to discern both good and evil? Be wise as a serpent and begin to notice the wickedness in apparently friendly people.

Tell us therefore, what thinkest thou? Is it lawful to give tribute unto Caesar, or not? But JESUS PERCEIVED THEIR WICKEDNESS, AND SAID, Why tempt ye me, ye hypocrites? Shew me the tribute money. And they brought unto him a penny. And he saith unto them, whose is this image and superscription? They say unto him, Caesar's. Then saith he unto them, Render therefore unto Caesar the things which are Caesar's; and unto God the things that are God's.

Matthew 22:17-21

5. Begin to sense the sweetness in the Word.

As you walk with the Lord, you will notice the sweetness of preaching and teaching. It becomes like honey to you. As you grow in the Lord, you will actually enjoy the Word of God. It will be sweet, enjoyable, exciting and exhilarating. You will even know different types of preaching that come from one man of God. Today, when I play the messages of Kenneth Hagin, I can sense his mood and I can even sense the type of anointing he is operating under. The Word of God is sweet to me.

You will also notice the dryness of the Word of God when it is being preached without the presence of God. There are a lot of de-anointed vessels preaching the Word of God today. When you are sensitive, you will see through it all in spite of the suave suits and numerous scriptures that are quoted.

I have refrained my feet from every evil way, that I might keep thy word. I have not departed from thy judgments: for thou hast taught me. How SWEET ARE THY WORDS unto my taste! Yea, sweeter than honey to my mouth!

Psalm 119:101-103

CHAPTER 20

Masters at Being Unpredictable

The wind bloweth where it listeth, and thou hearest the sound thereof, but canst not tell whence it cometh, and whither it goeth: so is EVERY ONE THAT IS BORN OF THE SPIRIT.

John 3:8

Serpents Are Wise Because They Are Unpredictable

A person who is born of the spirit will be as unpredictable and unreadable as the wind. This is bad news to the enemy.

Even though most snakes are harmless you can never tell what a snake is going to do. Will it strike? Will it run? Will it flee? Is it poisonous? Is it harmless? Is it dangerous? Can I kill it?

Being unpredictable creates a sense of mystery. No one can tell what you are going to do next. When you are unpredictable, it is difficult for people to neutralize the anointing on your life through familiarity.

Many pastors have the anointing on their lives cancelled by familiarity. Everyone knows what they are going to do next.

Defend yourself against familiarity by being unpredictable. Defend yourself against the bored yawns of your associates who have heard you preaching the same thing over and over again. Do the unexpected and you will create a fearsome reputation. No one will know what your next move is going to be. Both the Holy Spirit and Jesus are unpredictable in many of their operations.

Jesus Christ and Unpredictability

1. Jesus Christ was unpredictable when he was invited to the feast. At one point everyone thought He would come. At another time He said He would not come. In the end, He went to the feast and ministered powerfully. Notice how Jesus was wise as a serpent using the key of unpredictability.

Now the Jews' feast of tabernacles was at hand. His brethren therefore said unto him, Depart hence, and go into Judaea, that thy disciples also may see the works that thou doest.

For there is no man that doeth any thing in secret, and he himself seeketh to be known openly. If thou do these things, shew thyself to the world. For neither did his brethren believe in him.

Then Jesus said unto them, My time is not yet come: but your time is alway ready. The world cannot hate you; but me it hateth, because I testify of it, that the works thereof are evil. Go ye up unto this feast: I go not up yet unto this feast; for my time is not yet full come.

When he had said these words unto them, he abode still in Galilee. But WHEN HIS BRETHREN WERE GONE UP, THEN WENT HE ALSO UP UNTO THE FEAST, NOT OPENLY, but as it were in secret.

John 7:2-10

2. Jesus used the key of unpredictability in deciding where He would preach. People thought he would stay in town but He decided to go to the next village.

    And when they had found him, they said unto him, All men seek for thee. And he said unto them, Let us go into the next towns, that I may preach there also:for therefore came I forth.

    Mark 1:37-38

3. Jesus used the key of unpredictability in preaching. Everyone thought He would say something nice to make even more crowds come. He suddenly told them to drink His blood and eat His flesh and the crowds left Him.

    And he said, Therefore said I unto you, that no man can come unto me, except it were given unto him of my Father. From that time many of his disciples went back, and walked no more with him.

    John 6:65-66

4. Jesus used the key of unpredictability when He was at the peak of His ministry. Instead of continuing His ministry on earth, He decided to terminate it after three years and hand things over to the Comforter.

5. Jesus used the key of unpredictability in His healing ministry. It was difficult to tell what strategy He was going to use to minister to the next sick person. Sometimes he would lay hands on them. On others he would spit into sand. At other times he would just speak.

    Jesus used the key of unpredictability in His healing ministry. At times He would heal everybody and at other times He would heal only one person.

6. Jesus used the key of unpredictability in relation to eating and fasting. There were times everyone expected He and His disciples to fast; but they would eat. He fasted so much at the beginning of His ministry that only Moses could be compared with Him. He ate so much at other times that He was criticised for being a glutton.

7. Jesus used the key of unpredictability in His relationships. At times He only related with His disciples. At other times he moved around with the rich, famous and the corrupt. Everyone was shocked when He went to Zaccheus' house. Others were offended when He allowed Mary to wipe His feet with her hair.

The Holy Spirit and Unpredictability

1. The Holy Spirit is said to be so unpredictable that He is likened to the wind. You cannot tell where He is going or where He is coming from. You can also not tell what He is doing now and what He is going to do next. You simply cannot predict what the Holy Spirit is going to do. This is what makes Him awesome and fearful.

2. You cannot tell when the Holy Spirit is going to fall on people. The Holy Spirit fell on a hundred and twenty people in the Upper room after they had waited for forty days. But the Holy spirit fell on the disciples at Ephesus without them having to tarry for forty days.

3. You cannot tell what by method the Holy Spiri
   descend on people. The Holy Spirit came on the disc
   when Jesus breathed on them. The Holy Spirit cam
   the disciples in Samaria when Peter laid his hands on th
   The Holy Spirit came on Joshua when Moses laid his ha
   on him. The Holy Spirit came on the people in Corneli
   house whilst Peter was preaching.

4. You cannot tell what type of manifestation the Holy Spir
   is going to come up with. The Holy Spirit came on th
   disciples in the Upper Room with tongues of fire but since
   then He has not revealed any other tongues of fire.

5. You cannot tell whom the Holy Spirit is going to use. You
   cannot tell whom the Holy Spirit is going to work with. The
   Holy Spirit gives old men dreams and young men visions.
   The Holy Spirit gives women prophecies. So whom exactly
   is He going to use next? Babes and sucklings are also being
   anointed to bring forth praise. Who is the Holy Spirit going
   to use next?

CHAPTER 21

Masters at Working Alone

And when he had sent the multitudes away, he went up into a mountain apart to pray: and when the evening was come, HE WAS THERE ALONE.

Matthew 14:23

Serpents Are Wise Because
They Can Live And Work Alone

Snakes are often found on their own. Most of us have discovered a solitary snake somewhere in the garden before. A snake is not found with its mother, father or any other brothers. Snakes are experts at living alone. Snakes do not miss the company of others and do not seek the friendship and fellowship of other like-minded snakes.

Snakes are solitary animals that travel and live alone. Snakes have the ability to live in groups or to live alone for long times. There are things you cannot do in a group. You must also value being alone! Jesus Christ was alone many times. It was necessary that He was alone.

Every leader must accept that there are times he is alone in his decisions, in his ways and in his challenges. No one can understand you because no one is in your position! To be a leader is to be alone many times! To be wise as a serpent, you must learn to be alone when you have to be alone. You will notice how Jesus was alone many times. Because leaders are alone in their challenges, they are often alone in their victories. This is why leaders earn far more than anyone else.

Ten Times Jesus Was Alone

1. **Jesus was alone when he went to pray a great while before day.**

    And in the morning, rising up a great while before day, he went out, and departed into a solitary place, and there prayed.

    Mark 1:35

2. **Jesus was alone when He went into the wilderness to be tempted of the devil.**

    And Jesus being full of the Holy Ghost returned from Jordan, and was led by the Spirit into the wilderness,

131

being forty days tempted of the devil. And in those days he did eat nothing: and when they were ended, he afterward hungered.

Luke 4:1-2

3. Jesus was alone when he went up to the mountain to pray and choose his disciples.

And it came to pass in those days, that he went out into a mountain to pray, and continued all night in prayer to God. And when it was day, he called unto him his disciples: and of them he chose twelve, whom also he named apostles;

Luke 6:12-13

4. Jesus was alone when he was witnessing to the woman of Samaria.

There cometh a woman of Samaria to draw water: Jesus saith unto her, Give me to drink.

(For his disciples were gone away unto the city to buy meat.)

John 4:7-8

5. Jesus was alone when he came walking on the water to His disciples.

And in the fourth watch of the night Jesus went unto them, walking on the sea.

Matthew 14:25

6. Jesus was alone praying in Gethsemane.

And he went a little further, and fell on his face, and prayed, saying, O my Father, if it be possible, let this cup pass from me: nevertheless not as I will, but as thou wilt.

Matthew 26:39

7. **Jesus was alone when he was beaten before the Chief Priest and the elders.**

Then the high priest tore his robes, saying, "He has blasphemed! What further need do we have of witnesses? Behold, you have now heard the blasphemy; what do you think?" They answered and said, "He is deserving of death!"

Then they spat in His face and beat Him with their fists; and others slapped Him,"

Matthew 26:62-67 (NASB)

8. **Jesus was alone when he was interrogated by Pontius Pilate.**

And Jesus stood before the governor: and the governor asked him, saying, Art thou the King of the Jews? And Jesus said unto him, Thou sayest.

And when he was accused of the chief priests and elders, he answered nothing.

Then said Pilate unto him, Hearest thou not how many things they witness against thee?

Matthew 27:11-13

9. **Jesus was alone when He was beaten by the soldiers.**

Then the soldiers of the governor took Jesus into the Praetorium and gathered the whole Roman cohort around Him.

And they stripped Him, and put a scarlet robe on Him.

And after weaving a crown of thorns, they put it on His head, and a reed in His right hand; and they kneeled down before Him and mocked Him, saying, "Hail, King of the Jews!"

And they spat on Him, and took the reed and began to beat Him on the head.

Matthew 27:27-30 (NASB)

10. Jesus was alone on the cross. None of the other disciples was on the cross with him.

And when they had come to a place called Golgotha, which means Place of a Skull, they gave Him wine to drink mingled with gall; and after tasting it, He was unwilling to drink.

And when they had crucified Him, they divided up His garments among themselves, casting lots; and sitting down, they began to keep watch over Him there.

Matthew 27:33-36 (NASB)

Seven Things You Will Accomplish When You Are Alone with God

1. When you are alone with someone, you become close and intimate. There is a certain amount of closeness that you cannot have when you are having a group meeting. When you are alone with someone, you develop a far closer relationship than when you are in a group.

    You are not so close to God because you never have times with Him alone.

    That which was from the beginning, which we have heard, which we have seen with our eyes, which we have looked upon, and our hands have handled, of the Word of life; (For the life was manifested, and we have seen it, and bear witness, and shew unto you that eternal life, which was with the Father, and was manifested unto us;)

    1 John 1:1-2

2. When you are alone with someone, you develop a bond that cannot easily be acquired in public. Sometimes you cannot understand the bond that exists between people. These bonds are often created when people are together alone.

Endeavouring to keep the unity of the Spirit in the bond of peace.

Ephesians 4:3

3. When you are alone with someone, you acquire knowledge that you cannot acquire in public. You will know God in a much deeper way when you spend time alone with Him. Listen to Paul's prayer: "That I may know him, and the power of his resurrection, and the fellowship of his sufferings, being made conformable unto his death" (Philippians 3:10).

4. When you are alone with someone, you can receive an impartation that you cannot receive in public. The private impartation is often the most important impartation in your life. Through this impartation when you are alone, you can become very fruitful. Adam knew his wife, obviously not in public. "And Adam knew his wife again; and she bare a son, and called his name Seth: For God, said she, hath appointed me another seed instead of Abel, whom Cain slew" (Genesis 4:25). In 1988, I received an impartation of the anointing. It was 2.00am in the morning and I was all alone in my room in a remote town in Ghana.

5. When you are alone with someone, you can pray private prayers and make private petitions.

    Private prayers have promise of great reward. Jesus promised that we would have open rewards for secret prayers.

    But thou, when thou prayest, enter into thy closet, and when thou hast shut thy door, pray to thy Father which is in secret; and THY FATHER WHICH SEETH IN SECRET SHALL REWARD THEE OPENLY.

Matthew 6:6

6. When you are alone, you can fast and receive the greatest blessing of fasting when alone. The greatest blessing for fasting is revealed when you fast privately.

    But thou, when thou fastest, anoint thine head, and wash thy face; that thou appear not unto men to fast, but unto thy Father which is in secret: and THY FATHER, WHICH SEETH IN SECRET, SHALL REWARD THEE OPENLY.

    Matthew 6:17-18

7. The greatest blessing of giving is released when you give privately. As you can see, God has reserved special blessings for dealings that are done privately with Him. Don't shy away from being alone with God. It leads to the greatest blessing.

    But when thou doest alms, let not thy left hand know what thy right hand doeth: That thine alms may be in secret: and THY FATHER WHICH SEETH IN SECRET HIMSELF SHALL REWARD THEE OPENLY.

    Matthew 6:3-4

CHAPTER 22

Masters at Working With Others

And all that believed were together, ...

Acts 2:44

Serpents Are Wise Because of Their Ability To Live And Work With Others

Snakes are usually alone but can be found hibernating together in a communal spot. Over one hundred rattle snakes can be found together in a hole during winter. Sometimes in the mating season female snakes emit a pheromone that attract male cobras and this can also lead to a gathering of snakes in one area.

Amazingly, the same animal that is usually found alone can function with a large team of other snakes. To be wise as a serpent you must be able to function with a team. You must be able to delegate and you must be able to work with many other people. Some people are only able to work alone. That is not the wisdom of a serpent. You must be able to work alone but also be able to live and work with other people.

A snake charmer in Bangladesh once found 3,500 poisonous cobras and their eggs hidden underneath the floors of two suburban homes. Imagine that! 3,500 cobras flourishing under the boards of your living room!

Why is it important to live and work with others? Why is teamwork important? There are certain achievements that can only be done with a team. Solo efforts will not work! There was a time in ministry where I worked alone. Sometimes I worked with a couple of other people. But as I expanded and grew, I was forced to accept that I would work with a large team of people. Some achievements are simply impossible without a large team.

Climbing The Highest Mountain in Europe

I once visited the highest mountain in Europe. I was amazed at the dangerous and awesome snow peaks of these magnificent mountains. I could not help being afraid at different times of this experience. It is a place worth visiting! But what was even more amazing were the people who were climbing this mountain on foot. For some reason, thousands of people have a passion to climb these dangerous high mountains. They climb over glaciers (rivers of ice) that have steep crevices that go down hundreds of metres. They also climb vertical rock faces with ropes and ladders. It is just scary to look at! Every year, several people die trying to climb these mountains.

Strategy for Climbing The Highest Mountain in the World

Mount Everest which is the highest mountain in the world is far more dangerous. Mount Everest is almost double the height of European mountains at 8,848 metres high. Yet, every year, many people try to climb it, risking their very lives. What is amazing about climbing Mount Everest is the number of people that are needed to help one person climb Mount Everest.

Do you have any idea what it costs for one person to attempt to climb Mount Everest today? It will cost you between $30,000 and $100,000 to attempt to climb Mount Everest. It will take you four to ten weeks to climb Mount Everest. There is a reason for these huge costs! Several people will have to help you climb this mountain! A huge team of porters will have to help you climb the mountain. They will carry your equipment, food and oxygen for you. A huge team of guides, chefs, doctors, icefall doctors, helicopter pilots and so on will also be needed. No one person can go up the mountain on his own. It is a feat that is impossible on your own! This is where teamwork comes in. This is where the wisdom of being able to work in a group is essential.

For instance, the very first person who climbed Mount Everest was a man called Tenzing. He hired, organized and led a large team of over two hundred people for the journey to the top of the mountain. To get just two people to the summit, the team brought 10 high-altitude climbers. The team required almost 2.3 tonnes of equipment and food and these supplies were carried from Kathmandu on the backs of porters 290 kilometres up and down Himalayan ridges, and over rivers crossed by narrow rope-and-plank bridges to the base camp.

Another 40 porters with extensive mountain experience carried these supplies up the mountain. The strongest third of that team carried 340 kilograms of necessary equipment in to higher camps. Only Tenzing and three other porters had the strength and skill to go to camps near the summit.

The strategy was to allow one team to exhaust themselves just to get equipment up the mountain for the next group to use. Then two-man teams would work their way up the mountain, find the paths, cut steps and a path, and secure ropes. Tenzing, the man who reached the top of the mountain said:

"You do not climb a mountain like Everest by trying to race ahead on your own, or by competing with your comrades. You do it slowly and carefully, by unselfish teamwork. Certainly I wanted to reach the top myself; it was the thing I had dreamed of all my life. But if the lot fell to someone else I would take it like a man…"

What Strategy Do You Have for Climbing your Mountain?

Climbing a mountain was the passion of these unusual people. We all have mountains that we have desired to climb. Your mountain may be to build a large church! Your mountain may be a vision to be in the ministry. Your mountain may be what God has called you to do. You are going to have to learn how to work with people, especially if you have a call for great things.

Many people do not know how to work with others. Develop the art of working with different people. God wants to use you for much greater skills.

Seven People You Must Be Able to Work With

1. Develop the art of working with church members whom you preach to every Sunday. When you preach to people, it is not easy to discipline them, rebuke them and correct

them in the work place. A pastor has to combine the roles of being soft and understanding with being hard and demanding! That is a skill you have to develop if you are going to work with your church members.

2. Develop the art of working with unbelievers whose expertise you need. There are some die-hard sinners you will have to engage if you are to succeed. Sometimes people from other religions are better suited for certain jobs. You must master the art of working with certain people who do not believe the same things that you do. I have several people from other religions who work for me. In fact, one of my oldest workers is not a Christian at all.

3. Develop the art of working with people who are older than you. Some of the people you need most in life are older than you. With carefulness and respect, you will be able to work with those who are older than you.

4. Develop the art of working with lay people whom you do not pay. If you have to pay for everything you will be broke. Many good people want to volunteer their services. You must muster the art of getting them all involved. Amazingly, people feel so happy when they are given a little task to perform. Use the volunteers in your church and you will be amazed at their output.

5. Develop the art of working with women. If you are a man, you must develop the art of working with women without having sex with them. It is not as simple as it sounds and many ministries have been destroyed by the women who worked there. On the other hand, if you are a woman, you must develop the art of working with fellow women without quarrelling with them or being jealous. You must rise above pettiness and accept that you need their help.

6. Develop the art of working with people who do not like each other but who need to work together. Paul had this problem with two ladies, Euodias and Syntyche. He said to them, "I beseech Euodias, and beseech Syntyche, that

they be of the same mind in the Lord" (Philippians 4:2). People who get along with you may not get along with each other. The fact that they do not get along with each other can make you lose one of them. You must fight to work with everyone whom God has destined to be with you.

7. Develop the art of working with technical people. It is important to know how to work with technical people because they have a way of contradicting the mission with their technicalities. Lawyers can write a constitution for a church that will destroy the church in future. Architects and engineers can destroy the pastor's ministry by coming up with impractical ideas that can never be financed or finished. I am always able to recognize church buildings that will never be finished. The design is so bad, so impractical and expensive! You must develop the art of working with these people in such a way that they do not destroy you. You will do this by knowing a little about everything that is being done. Do not assume that you cannot understand what these professionals are saying. Open your mind, listen carefully and ask many questions. Do not black out and let them say you cannot understand. You will understand everything if you apply your mind to it!

CHAPTER 23

Masters of
Radical Change

But we all ...are changed into the same image ...

2 Corinthians 3:18

Serpents Are Wise Because of Their Ability To Shed Their Skin

Snakes grow quickly and most of them can kill from the day they are born! Imagine that! Snakes are able to be independent from birth.

Snakes normally shed their skin to allow for growth. Whenever you see the shed skin of a snake you are seeing the evidence of growth and development.

Snakes undergo this major and dramatic manoeuvre of shedding their skin to prompt and bring about growth.

But we all, with open face beholding as in a glass the glory of the Lord, are changed into the same image from glory to glory, even as by the Spirit of the Lord.

2 Corinthians 3:18

Every minister must be a master of radical change. To be wise as a serpent, you have to undergo radical change, shed your skin and have a completely new presentation. Throughout my ministry, I have experienced several radical changes. I pastored a small church in a classroom. Then I pastored a church in a corridor. Then I became a pastor of a church in a canteen. Then I became a full time pastor of a church in a cinema hall. After some years, I became a Bishop in a cathedral overseeing many churches. Then I moved forward and became an evangelist conducting crusades. After that I became a pastor of a youth church.

When a snake changes its skin it is still the same snake with the same vision. Because of its new skin it is able to expand and grow and do greater works. When it sheds its skin, it is able to overcome bigger animals and have bigger meals. It is probably a more dangerous animal because of the radical change. Don't be afraid of radical changes as the Lord moves you forward.

Four Radical Changes
in the Ministry of Jesus

1. The radical change in Bethlehem: Jesus Christ underwent a major transformation. He came down from heaven and was born as a baby.

2. The radical change in Nazareth: Jesus Christ grew up as a normal young man, silently learning and humbly obeying His parents.

3. The radical change in Galilee: Jesus Christ was transformed radically from a quiet and humble carpenter's apprentice to a radical preacher with miracles, signs and wonders. Galilee was the region that had cities like Capernaum, Chorazin and Bethsaida. It was in these cities that Jesus performed awesome miracles. This was the third phase of His ministry. The change from Nazareth to Galilee was dramatic. In Nazareth, Jesus was a quiet unassuming person, living a normal carpenter's life. But then He underwent a radical change and moved forward with a completely new presentation. When a snake sheds its skin, it dramatically reveals a brand new shining glistening coat. A new day is born and new things are going to come forth. Radical changes are working.

4. The radical change in Jerusalem: The ministry of Jesus Christ underwent a radical change. He was transformed from a radical, outgoing and invincible preacher into a humble lamb. As a humble lamb, He allowed himself to be subjected to interrogation, torture and crucifixion. This part of His ministry was quite different from Galilee, Nazareth or Bethlehem. It was to be the last radical change on earth.

Four Keys to Radical Change
in Your Ministry

1. Make radical changes by carefully listening to the voice of the Holy Spirit. Following the will of God will guarantee a radical change in your life and ministry.

2. Make radical changes in your ministry by taking major decisions. Radical changes are brought about by taking major decisions. Changing the time of a church service from 7.30am to 8.00am is not a major decision and it will not bring about a major change to your ministry. Minor decisions will only lead to minor changes in the ministry. Deciding to acquire a church building is a major decision that will lead to a radical change in your ministry.

3. Make the radical changes of your life and ministry without ever departing from your original calling. It is very dangerous to step away from the principles of the word of God and the call of God. If you have been called to be a pastor, you are likely to be a pastor all your life. You may pastor different groups of people but that calling will never go away. If you are called to be a prophet that calling will stay with you. The gifts and calling of God are without repentance.

    You can never set aside John 3:16 and the purpose for which Christ came to shed His blood. Jesus did not shed His blood for us so that we would be successful. He shed His blood for us to save us from our sins. God did not send His son to this world to make us rich or to give us a good life in America. Do not change the gospel! God sent His Son into the world that we might not perish. The whole church must not depart from these foundations. Departing from these foundations is not a radical change but a radical deterioration.

4. Make the radical changes without violating spiritual laws. Do not violate, disobey or dishonour your spiritual fathers because you are making a radical change in your ministry. Do not break the church you have belonged to for years when you make a radical change. The radical change I am talking about does not include disloyalty and treachery. Judas decided to sell his master, Jesus Christ! That was not a radical change. That was radical destruction. As you read this book, may God give you radical upward and forward changes in your life and ministry.

MASTERS OF NON-DEPENDENT LIVING

... living alone and growing larger

MASTERS OF INNER POWER

... full of venom, spitting venom

MASTERS OF THE POWER OF THE MOUTH

... swallowing a crocodile

MASTERS OF OVERCOMING HANDICAPS

... without legs, climbing a tree

MASTERS OF GIVING THEMSELVES WHOLLY

... *coiling completely around an antelope*

MASTERS OF MANOEUVRES

... *jumping, flying and striking*

MASTERS OF SURVIVAL

... living in the desert sands

MASTERS OF CONTENTMENT

... content with one meal a year

MASTERS OF PATIENCE

... waiting patiently by the river side

MASTERS OF FRUGALITY

... nothing is wasted. Swallowing the head, horns, hoofs and legs

MASTERS OF HIDING AND FLOURISHING

... can you see? ...hiding in the leaves.

MASTERS OF SELF-DEFENCE

... defending itself

MASTERS OF OVERCOMING DEMONS

... swallowing another snake

MASTERS OF REPUTATION

... deadly fangs loaded with venom

MASTERS OF LIVING PEACEABLY WITH MEN

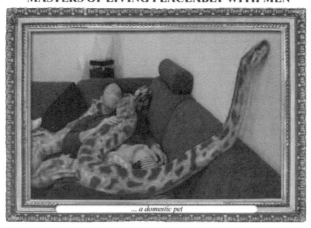

... a domestic pet

MASTERS AT SUBDUING SPOUSES

... swallowing a spouse after mating

MASTERS OF SPEED

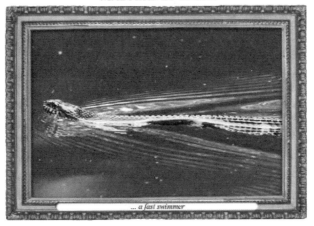

... a fast swimmer

MASTERS AT OPERATING BY THE SENSES

... powerful sensors in the forked tongue

MASTERS AT BEING UNPREDICTABLE

... finding its way through the sewage pipes and into the toilet bowl

MASTERS AT WORKING ALONE

... alone in the desert

MASTERS AT WORKING WITH OTHERS

... living with others

MASTERS OF RADICAL CHANGE

... shedding skin, taking up new colours

Notes

Excerpts taken from:

1. *A mass of interesting facts about animals*. Retrieved from http://buy1or2.com/keep-kleen/animals.html Web 21 March 2017

2. *Super strong slithering snakes*. Retrieved from http://taketheshot-nick.blogspot.com/2011/04/super-strong-slithering-snakes.html Web 21 March 2017

3. *Snakes*. Retrieved from https://books.google.com.gh/books?id=JbqNAwAAQBAJ&pg=PT78&lpg=PT78&dq=%22Snakes+do+not+chew+their+food.%22&source=bl&ots=WiU6y4PumT&sig=yZ8zAtgySyfGR4mAPcIaWBeN7Ps&hl=en&sa=X&ved=0ahUKEwirkpSx0ODSAhWhK8AKHd7SAZ0Q6AEIMjAF#v=onepage&q=%22Snakes%20do%20not%20chew%20their%20food.%22&f=false Web 21 March 2017

4. *The snake skull (head)*. Retrieved from http://bjeromedesilva-snakelover.blogspot.com/p/snake-skull-head.html Web 21 March 2017

5. *Cobras, kraits, seasnakes, death adders, and relatives (elapidae)*. Retrieved from http://www.encyclopedia.com/environment/encyclopedias-almanacs-transcripts-and-maps/cobras-kraits-seasnakes-death-adders-and-relatives-elapidae Web 21 March 2017

6. *Animal stories: snakes*. Retrieved from https://thehimalayantimes.com/entertainment/animal-stories-snakes/ Web 21 March 2017

7. *Reptiles guide - pit vipers*. Retrieved from https://nwseed.com/content/reptiles/Crotalinae.html Web 21 March 2017

8. *Snake*. Retrieved from https://en.wikipedia.org/wiki/Snake Web 21 March 2017

9. *There is no "I" in "T-E-A-M-W-O-R-K"!* Retrieved from http://www.academia.edu/3610233/There_is_no_I_in_T-E-A-M-W-O-R-K_ Web 21 March 2017